Curiosity in a
Data-Filled World

Data Literacy for Everyone

Dave Wells

Technics Publications
SEDONA, ARIZONA

115 Linda Vista, Sedona, AZ 86336 USA
https://www.TechnicsPub.com

Edited by Steve Hoberman
Cover design by Lorena Molinari

First Printing 2026

Copyright © 2026 by Dave Wells

ISBN, print ed.   9798898160791
ISBN, Kindle ed.   9798898160807
ISBN, PDF ed.   9798898160814

Library of Congress Control Number: 2026937519

Contents

Foreword

You leave the house in the morning and get into your car.

Before you even shift into drive, the car reminds you to fasten your seatbelt. That's data.

You pull onto the road. Your GPS shows traffic congestion on your usual route. It estimates drive time. It predicts arrival time. It offers an alternate route that could save six minutes. That's data.

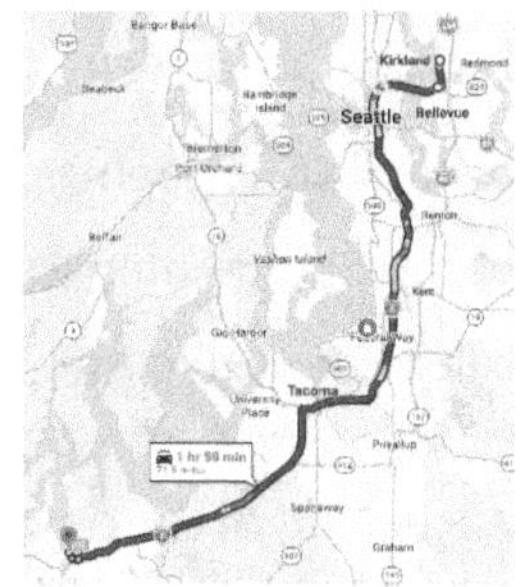

On the dashboard, a digital display reports your speed, direction, fuel level, and real-time fuel consumption. It shows average miles per gallon (MPG) since your last fill-up. It

calculates how many miles you have left before you'll need gas again. That's more data.

You glance at the outside temperature. You notice the "eco" indicator light. You adjust your speed. The car responds. More data.

You arrive at the parking garage. An LED sign announces that floors one and two are full, floor three has 42 spaces available, and floor four has 96. You choose a level. That choice is shaped by data.

And you haven't even started your work day yet.

Once you do, data will be everywhere. It may show up in spreadsheets, schedules, dashboards, orders, test results, production reports, customer counts, attendance logs, and performance metrics. Whatever your work involves, data plays a role. But we'll come back to that.

At the end of the day, you return to the parking garage and prepare to drive home. Again, the GPS reports routes, delays, and estimated travel time. Traffic has shifted. Your options have changed.

On the way home, you stop at the store to buy groceries. You look at prices. You scan nutrition labels to compare ingredients, calories, and serving sizes. You make choices based on what you see.

At self-checkout, you enter your customer number. Now you're providing data. As each item is scanned, a voice announces the price and any discount you earned as a registered customer. The system does more than inform you. It records your purchases, linking them to your account, and updating your profile.

When the transaction is complete, a receipt prints. It itemizes each product, its price, the discount applied, the tax charged, the total cost, and the total savings. It reports fuel discount points earned and your current balance. All of this is data as a summary of decisions, translated into numbers.

You leave the store. The GPS updates traffic conditions and recalculates travel time. The dashboard displays speed, direction, fuel level, and fuel efficiency. You decide to stop for gas.

At the pump, the display shows the price per gallon and the octane rating for regular, premium, and super-premium options. You select one. As the numbers tick upward,

gallons and total cost increase in real time. You pump just over 14.6 gallons for a total of $59.96. The transaction ends with another receipt—more records, more summaries, more data.

You pull away from the pump. The GPS adjusts again. Traffic has changed. Your arrival time updates.

And the data just keeps coming.

Most of us do not think of this as "working with data." It feels like driving, shopping, planning, and deciding. Yet nearly every step is shaped by measurements, counts, categories, scores, predictions, and records. Data influences routes. Data reports performance.

Data tracks purchases. Data accumulates quietly in the background.

Much of this data passes without deliberate thought. It becomes information only when we pause to interpret it—when we ask what it means, whether it is reliable, and how it should influence our choices. Without that pause, data influences decisions without being examined.

We live in a world saturated with data, yet very few of us were taught how to work with it thoughtfully. We learned to read words. We learned to write sentences. We practiced arithmetic. But rarely were we taught how to question a metric, interpret a trend, weigh evidence, or recognize when data deserves caution.

That gap is why I wrote this book.

The book is written for anyone who lives in a world surrounded by data. That means it is written for you.

You do not need to be a data professional, a technical expert, or a numbers person to benefit from it. You only need curiosity and a willingness to think carefully about the data that flows through daily life. Some chapters will feel immediately familiar. Others may introduce ideas that stretch your perspective. Every section supports growth in awareness, judgment, and understanding.

The early chapters focus on awareness, including recognizing how often data appears in ordinary moments and how it influences decisions. The middle chapters explore habits of interpretation:

comparison, pattern recognition, judgment, and communication. As those habits develop, data becomes information. Data takes on meaning through context, definitions, and careful attention. Later sections bring structure to these ideas by outlining the knowledge areas that support strong data literacy across personal, professional, and civic contexts.

You can read this book straight through, or you can move selectively. If you are most interested in practical habits, you may spend more time with the chapters on thinking, learning, and curiosity. If you want a structured summary of key concepts, the Data Literacy Body of Knowledge (DLBOK) in the appendix provides a concise reference organized by domain. The glossary offers clear definitions of key terms and can be consulted whenever you want clarification.

The aim is thoughtful engagement with data. As you read, you may begin to notice data differently. You may pause more often before accepting a number at face value. You may ask better questions. You may recognize patterns you once overlooked. Over time, these small shifts accumulate.

Data literacy develops gradually. It strengthens through attention, reflection, and use. This book is designed to support that process across a lifetime.

PART I

Data Literacy as a Life Skill

Data is now part of daily life. Fitness trackers record movement, banking apps track spending, navigation tools predict arrival times, and headlines turn statistics into stories. Much of this data sits quietly in the background, shaping how people understand what is going on and what to do next. It affects how we plan, how we decide, and how we make sense of the world around us.

Data literacy is the set of skills that let people read, question, and use data in thoughtful ways. It is often described as something needed for school or work, but reaches into many other parts of life. It touches family decisions, personal routines, and community life. It affects how people think, form opinions, and participate in the world.

> *Reading and writing were the essential skills of the last century. Working with data has become an essential skill for this one.*

Children growing up today will enter adulthood in a world where data flows constantly, decisions happen quickly, and predictions and recommendations shape many choices. When we develop these skills early in life, they become natural throughout life.

This part of the book looks at how data shows up in everyday life and how data literacy begins earlier than most people realize, often taking shape through curiosity, comparison, and questions in childhood.

ONE

Data Literacy in Everyday Life

Data is now part of the structure of daily life. It appears in measurements, totals, grades, forecasts, and routes. Cars report fuel efficiency and distance. Receipts describe purchases and points earned. Nutrition labels summarize ingredients and proportions. Report cards and dashboards translate activity into scores and averages. What once required deliberate record-keeping now arrives automatically, often without notice.

Data literacy begins with a simple awareness of data. Increasingly, decisions both large and small draw on data. From *Is the commute faster this way?* to *Can we adjust the budget?* to *Is that headline worth believing?* data keeps showing up whether we invited it or not.

Data literacy is how people make sense of data.
It matters because data shows up in every corner of life.

Data literacy is how people make sense of it. It's the ability to read, interpret, explain, and question information presented as numbers, categories, ratings, dashboards, or simple tallies. In the same way that language literacy lets us understand words and ideas, data literacy lets us understand counts, comparisons, and trends. Data literacy matters because it shows up in every corner of life long before it becomes a workplace requirement.

From reading and writing to working with data

For most of history, literacy has meant reading and writing words. Language literacy is still essential as books, e-mails, contracts, and signs are here to stay. But today, many messages arrive as charts, statistics, rankings, and scores. *How many?*, *How much?*, and *Compared to what?* are now part of ordinary conversation.

Working with data doesn't require advanced software. It often begins with the simple act of asking what something means. A line graph showing rising costs, a score showing "creditworthiness," and a dashboard showing case counts make sense only if we know how to interpret them: *What is being measured? Over what time period? Against which baseline? With what degree of certainty?*

These questions are increasingly necessary because automated systems are no longer background utilities. AI models recommend products, filter news, set prices, score risk, and decide eligibility. Their outputs may look like facts, but they are built from assumptions, rules, and training data. Being literate means recognizing that recommendations and predictions are not neutral—they are arguments about what might matter.

Data literacy is the modern extension of reading, writing, and reasoning. It doesn't require special technical skills, but it does require thinking skills.

Data in everyday life

Data doesn't arrive in tidy tables. It comes as notifications, charts, ratings, totals, estimates, and warnings. It also comes as nudges: subtle suggestions engineered to shape behavior. The environments where data shows up are familiar, even if the mechanisms behind them are not.

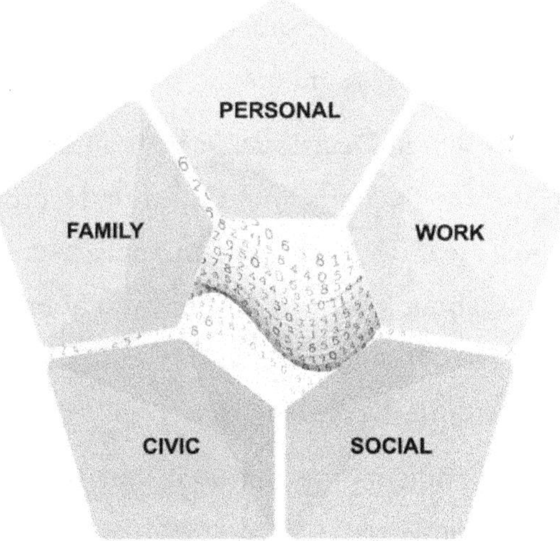

Figure 1. Dimensions of Data in Everyday Life

- **Personal—Health, Money, and Time:** Sleep trackers, nutrition apps, banking alerts, and budgeting dashboards provide nudges and summaries. Some help; some simply remind you that you've been ignoring subscriptions for too long.

- **Work—Data on the Job:** Queue lengths, service metrics, safety logs, audits, forecasts, and key performance indicators (KPIs) appear in workplaces of all kinds. Some help coordinate, some hold people accountable, and some simply request more spreadsheets.

- **Social—What Spreads and Why:** Likes, shares, follows, views, and rankings shape what people notice and how they perceive others. Recommendation feeds quietly influence attention, taste, and identity.

- **Civic—Headlines and Dashboards:** Public dashboards summarize disease rates, air quality, water levels, and voting results. Headlines convert statistics into stories about the world—and sometimes the stories are more dramatic than the numbers.

- **Family—Shared Decisions:** Parents and caregivers navigate growth charts, immunization records, school dashboards, and learning apps. Data can support decisions about health, education, and household routines, and it sometimes starts the arguments that those decisions depend on.

All of these environments are different, but the skills used to navigate them overlap.

Clearing up misconceptions

Data literacy is often misunderstood in three ways:

- **Misconception 1:** "It's about charts and dashboards." Visuals matter, but literacy includes questioning where data came from, how categories were defined, what's missing, and whether the information actually supports the conclusions being presented.

- **Misconception 2:** "It's a technical skill for specialists." Experts need technical depth, but basic literacy belongs to everyone. People make data-influenced decisions long before they ever see a dashboard at work.

- **Misconception 3:** "It's mostly workplace stuff." Work matters, but so do family decisions, civic participation, and personal habits. Many of the most important decisions (financial, educational, medical, and democratic) happen outside workplaces altogether.

Learning to think with data

Data literacy is grounded in how we think. Three kinds of thinking show up frequently:

- **Critical thinking**: asking what the evidence really shows and what assumptions might be shaping the conclusion.

- **Statistical thinking**: recognizing that numbers vary and that a single figure rarely tells the whole story.

- **Systems thinking**: understanding that events have context and that most outcomes are influenced by more than one factor.

For most people, these are not formal methods or academic disciplines. They appear as habits. Pausing before reacting. Asking how solid a number seems. Wondering whether something changed for a reason or by coincidence. Considering what else might be influencing the result.

Data literacy is fundamentally about thinking:
Becoming less easily confused, more appropriately
curious, and better equipped for the world we live in.

Learning to think with data doesn't happen through lectures. It develops through practice—comparing changes over time, noticing patterns, questioning claims, and discussing decisions with others. The skills accumulate quietly and spread across life.

Data literacy helps people avoid confusion, approach data with curiosity, and navigate the world we live in. You don't have to be a numbers expert to be data literate.

Two

Data in Everyday Life: Three Perspectives

Most days don't announce themselves as data-rich. They just happen. You check how long your commute will take, whether your kid's school app has new messages, how many emails piled up overnight, and whether the news says the air is safe to breathe. Later, you glance at a dashboard at work, skim a headline about public health, and compare prices before buying dinner.

None of this feels like "working with data," but that's exactly what it is: information, interpretation, judgment, and small decisions layered throughout the day. What changes from moment to moment is context: sometimes you're deciding for yourself, sometimes with others, and sometimes as part of a much larger community. This chapter looks at three of those contexts: the personal, the work, and the societal. Same person, same brain, same habits—different stakes, audiences, and consequences.

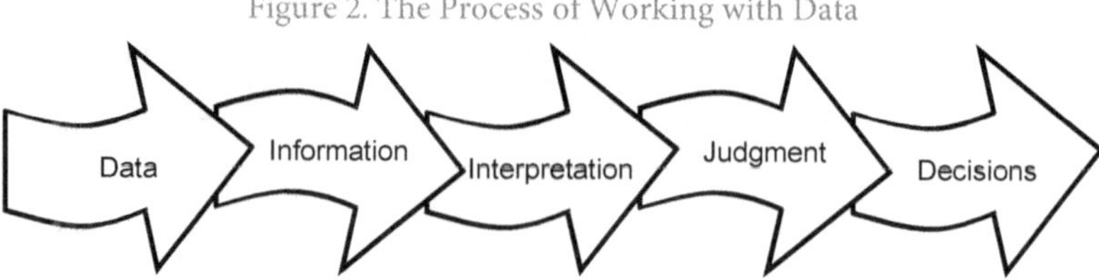

Figure 2. The Process of Working with Data

The personal perspective: my information, my choices

The personal perspective is about the data that follows you around: health, money, attention, time, and preferences. It comes from step counters, calendars, bank apps, sleep trackers, news summaries, and whatever other digital assistants you've allowed into your life.

Most personal decisions blend data with instinct. A sleep tracker might say you had a terrible night, but if you feel fine, you might ignore it. A budgeting app might warn you that "Eating Out" is over budget, but you decide that lunch with a friend was worth it. Numbers are clues and suggestions; people decide what actually matters. Personal data literacy shows up in little habits:

- Asking where numbers came from before trusting them

- Comparing patterns over time instead of reacting to one weird spike

- Noticing how recommendations made by AI nudge attention, purchases, and mood

> *Numbers make suggestions. People decide what actually matters. Think of automated predictions and recommendations as advice, not as instructions.*

Personal data tools are increasingly designed to predict and guide choices. Credit scoring, price personalization, eligibility checks, and recommendation feeds don't just report information, they shape options. Being literate means thinking of recommendations as advice, not as instructions.

Figure 3. Recommendations Try to Shape Behaviors

TOO GOOD TO REFUSE!
GET 50% OFF
YOUR ORDER +
+ FREE SHIPPING!
LIMITED TIME ONLY!
BUY
SHOP NOW
THIS OFFER WON'T LAST LONG!

Personal data also involves boundaries. Deciding what to track, what to share, and when to say "no thank you" is part of the skill set. Convenience is nice, but not every tap, swipe, or photo needs to become a permanent record somewhere.

The work perspective: data on the job

Nearly every job now involves information: some measured, some counted, some summarized, and some predicted. A customer service rep sees tickets and satisfaction scores. A facilities technician sees logs, gauges, and inspection reports. Office staff see spreadsheets and schedules. Managers see KPIs, forecasts, and risk reports. Data and AI professionals see…well, too much of everything.

The point isn't that everyone does the same work. It's that everyone uses data to coordinate action. Service workers prioritize queues, tradespeople make operational judgments, office workers reconcile records, and leaders make decisions about staffing, strategy, and impact.

Working with data brings responsibilities.
Accuracy, confidentiality, fairness, and consent are not
abstract topics. They shape what happens to real people.

Workplace data literacy shows up in questions such as:
- Is this information fit for what I'm trying to do?
- What action does it suggest?
- What happens if it's wrong?

And increasingly:
- What is the AI system assuming, and when should I disagree with it?

Work also involves responsibility. Many jobs require handling data about other people, including students, patients, customers, employees, or residents. Accuracy, confidentiality, fairness, and consent are more than abstract ethical topics; they shape what happens to real people in real systems.

The societal perspective: public life, institutions, and power

Some data isn't about individuals or workplaces at all. It describes communities, regions, and entire societies. These numbers appear in public dashboards, news graphics, policy debates, and election coverage, often accompanied by urgent headlines and colorful charts.

Common public indicators include unemployment rates, test scores, crime statistics, hospital capacity, emissions data, polling results, and budget allocations. Forecasting models show up too—predicting storms, disease outbreaks, and election outcomes.

Institutions decide which numbers become visible and which remain quietly hidden.
Public data literacy requires curiosity and understanding that numbers can illuminate or obscure, depending on who uses them and why.

Reading public data responsibly is partly about comprehension and partly about context. People ask:

- How is this being measured?
- Who is included, and who is not?
- Which comparisons are fair, and which are misleading?
- What uncertainty is being hidden behind a single number?

Storytelling in public life involves power. Institutions decide which numbers become visible and which ones quietly remain in spreadsheets. Headlines emphasize what will capture attention. Dashboards emphasize what leaders want to manage. Definitions determine who counts and who doesn't.

Public data literacy doesn't require cynicism. It requires curiosity plus a healthy understanding that numbers can illuminate or obscure depending on who uses them and why.

One day, many perspectives

Nobody wakes up in the "personal context," commutes into the "work context," and ends the day in the "societal context." The three mingle constantly. The same person may compare grocery prices at lunch (personal), reconcile competing records at work (professional), and research an initiative on the ballot after dinner (civic).

The things that change across perspectives are the stakes, the time, and the power dynamics. The underlying skill set is consistent across all perspectives. At home, a misinterpretation might cost a few dollars or a few hours. At work, it might delay a project or misdirect resources. In civic life, it can shape communities, institutions, and public trust.

The encouraging part: the same core habits travel well. Noticing patterns, questioning sources, comparing alternatives, reading visuals carefully, and making informed decisions apply in all three settings. Data literacy is portable. It goes where you go.

PART II

Working with Data

Data literacy comes into focus when people begin working directly with data. Most of that work is quiet and ordinary. It looks like noticing a balance on a statement, checking a label on a form, glancing at a chart in a meeting, or comparing last month's numbers to this month's numbers. The moment someone asks, *What does this tell me?* data stops being trivial and becomes something to handle, question, and use.

> *Data literacy depends on attention, judgment,*
> *and the ability to connect information with real situations.*

Working with data involves a handful of recurring moves. People notice and interpret records and measures. They ask whether the information is reliable, complete, and relevant. They use what they find to make choices about health, money, time, and responsibilities. And they communicate what they learn through numbers, visuals, and words, as part of conversations and shared decisions. None of this depends on specialized tools. It depends on attention, judgment, and the ability to connect information with real situations.

This part of the book walks through those practices step by step: finding meaning in data, questioning what it suggests, using it in decisions, and communicating it clearly. The purpose is to show how data literacy capabilities support understanding, decision making, and action.

Finding Meaning in Data

Data is often described as "facts and figures," but the phrase makes it sound cold and impartial, like something stored in filing cabinets or spreadsheets for its own amusement. In real life, data is better understood as recorded experience: snapshots of what happened, captured in a way that it can be reviewed and revisited when needed.

Receipts record what was bought and what was paid. Calendars record what was planned. Sleep apps record when you gave up and looked at your phone at 3 a.m. Each record is a tiny trace of life that becomes useful only when someone asks a question: *How much? When? How often? Compared to what?*

Data is best understood as recorded experience: snapshots of what happened.
Data records are selective. They show some things and ignore others.

Most everyday data appears quietly, without announcements and in forms other than dashboards. It's in notes, reminders, logs, counts, and icons. Sometimes it's deliberate (tracking expenses), and sometimes it's automatic (a phone that insists you've walked fewer steps today). Meaning appears when patterns are noticed and questions are asked: *What does this describe? What might it explain?*

Understanding data as a record of experience makes it feel natural and familiar. It also highlights a truth that becomes important later: records are selective. They show some things and ignore others, and the choices involved are rarely neutral.

Personal and family information: records that follow us

Some of the most influential data in life is personal: names, addresses, immunization history, grades, test scores, employment records, credit files, account information, etc. These records tend to persist. They travel from school to school, clinic to clinic, and system to system. Unlike a conversation that fades, a record can be copied, shared, stored, and reused.

Here's a real-life example:

A parent logs in to a school portal to check a lunch balance. Thirty minutes later, they've reviewed attendance, assignments, test scores, and five unexplained status codes. The student, currently eating cereal, has no idea their academic life is being parsed like a quarterly earnings report.

Records like this shape decisions about placement, support, eligibility, billing, and sometimes opportunity. Data literacy here includes knowing what information exists, where it lives, how accurate it is, and who has access to it. Small mistakes, such as a misspelled name, an outdated address, or a missing update, can have surprisingly lasting consequences if left uncorrected.

> *Personal data literacy includes knowing what data exists, where it exists, how accurate it is, and who has access to it.*

Families often act as stewards of this information. They complete forms, manage portals, update records, and provide consent on behalf of children or elders. Understanding what is being captured and why makes it easier to spot errors, ask questions, and advocate when something doesn't look right.

Counts and measures: time, money, quantities, and scores

A lot of the work of finding meaning with data begins with simple counting: hours worked, steps walked, money spent, pages read, chores completed, days absent, miles driven, and points scored. None of these requires analytics software. They require only that we notice them and record them.

People routinely track:

- **Time**: Calendars, timers, schedules, commute length.
- **Money**: Balances, bills, expenses, subscriptions.
- **Quantities**: Groceries, medication refills, fuel, anything that comes in packs.
- **Scores**: Credit, test results, performance ratings, game points.

These measures help answer familiar questions: *Can we afford this? Is this typical? Is this improving? Is this urgent?*

Finding meaning requires context. A high grocery bill makes sense if it's the week before a holiday. A lower test score matters differently if the student is exhausted from a school play. A "good" credit score means one thing for a loan and something else for renting an apartment.

Figure 4. Finding Meaning in Data

Data in digital life: traces, metrics, and nudges

Digital systems are enthusiastic collectors. They tally clicks, scrolls, views, pauses, watch time, streaks, likes, and curious moments of hesitation. These traces are then transformed into engagement metrics, recommendation signals, and behavioral profiles. None of this is accidental. A streak counter in a learning app encourages practice. A "days active" badge encourages loyalty. Autoplay encourages surrender. These metrics may look like measurements, but they often function as nudges: design choices intended to influence behavior.

Digital systems use metrics to influence behavior.
Digital data literacy involves recognizing when metrics are designed to persuade.

Digital data literacy begins with recognizing this double life: metrics can inform and persuade. A streak might reflect genuine progress or simply consecutive logins. A "recommended for you" list might reflect taste, or just a system that is trying to keep you scrolling. Meaning requires asking gently skeptical questions: *What is being counted? What is being ignored? Whose goals are these metrics serving?*

Not everything that is measured is important.
Not everything that is important is measured.

Simple sense-making: patterns, comparisons, and change

Once data is recognized, the next step is sense-making: noticing patterns, making comparisons, and tracking changes over time. This is the foundation on which complex reasoning is built.

Micro-sense-making happens constantly:

- Why are grocery bills higher in September?
- Why are the kids more tired on Tuesdays?
- Why did the dog food run out faster this month?

These observations don't require statistics; they require curiosity and a bit of consistency. Meaning accumulates when someone checks back more than once.

---

*Making sense of data involves
curiosity, consistency, and restraint.*

The temptation, of course, is to react to single data points: one high bill, one bad night of sleep, one surprising test score. Sense-making encourages patience: wait for a pattern, compare like with like, and ask if the context changed. It also rewards restraint, a skill rarely praised but frequently useful.

Safety, privacy, and consent basics

Because so much personal data is now digital, understanding safety, privacy, and consent has become a practical necessity. Even very young children can grasp that some information is private, that not everyone should see everything, and that sharing something online is different from whispering it to a friend.

Families negotiate privacy constantly: *Can I post this photo? Can I share this information with the school? Who sees what on this device?* Adults face similar questions with higher stakes: financial accounts, insurance applications, health records, and subscription platforms with terms longer than most short stories.

Figure 5. Awareness Before Consent – Questions that Protect Your Data

Data literacy includes understanding:

- What information is collected
- Who collects it
- Why they want it
- Where it goes
- How long it stays
- Who benefits from sharing it

Consent is about so much more than granting permission; it's about awareness and choice.

Foundations across ages

The abilities in this chapter, like recognizing data, noticing patterns, asking questions, comparing values, and practicing some degree of privacy judgment, emerge early and evolve through life.

Data literacy doesn't begin with tools and technologies.
It begins with noticing things.

Children count blocks and compare who has more. Students track grades and time. Adults monitor budgets, sleep, chores, dashboards, and appointments. Workers rely on information to coordinate and decide. Communities use data to argue, advocate, persuade, and reform.

The contexts change. The consequences change. The stakes change. But the underlying capacities stay remarkably portable.

Data literacy doesn't begin with tools and technologies; it begins with noticing things. And it grows when noticing becomes questioning, and questioning becomes understanding.

FOUR

Questioning Data and Meaning

Data rarely arrives with instructions. A chart pops up in the news, a number appears in a dashboard, or a statistic makes its way into conversation. Suddenly, we're expected to believe it, explain it, or act on it. Questioning data is how we slow things down just long enough to understand what's being shown and whether it deserves to influence decisions.

Most data encounters start quietly. You see a number, a spike on a graph, a headline claiming "screen time is up," or a dashboard warning that backlog is "critical." The moment of data-awareness is quick. The next move, questioning or accepting, matters a lot more.

Questioning slows things down to understand the data
and whether it should influence decisions.
Curiosity is active thinking about data and a healthy
orientation to working with data.

Curiosity turns passive consumption into active thinking. Useful questions are rarely complicated. They sound like:

- Where did this come from?
- Who decided this was worth measuring?
- What counts and what doesn't?
- Is anything missing?

Curiosity isn't cynicism in disguise; it's a healthy orientation. It keeps meaning from being assigned too quickly and opens space for context, nuance, and better decisions.

Reasoning from data to evidence

Data becomes evidence when someone uses it to support a conclusion. Not all data does this equally well. Strong evidence is usually:

- Numerous enough to represent more than a handful of cases
- Relevant to the situation being considered
- Transparent about how it was collected and summarized
- Consistent across time, groups, and methods

Weak evidence is often small, selective, or accidental. One glowing review does not prove that a product is life-changing. One personal story does not prove that a policy works. A single month of sales data cannot reveal a trend, no matter how satisfying the line chart looks.

Strong evidence is representative.
Weak evidence is selective.

Reasoning also means considering more than the first explanation that comes to mind. When outcomes change, it's tempting to credit the nearest cause: "Sales went up because we redesigned the website!" This, however, ignores other influences like seasonal demand, a competitor's outage, a viral TikTok review, or the simple fact that February had fewer days than March.

Reality is usually driven by combinations of influences, not a single cause. Reasoning well means giving those combinations a chance to be seen.

Correlation, cause, and bias

Graphs love to make two lines rise and fall together. It's visually convincing. Unfortunately, correlation is the master illusion of data interpretation: proximity masquerading as explanation.

A favorite example: Ice cream sales and drowning deaths rise together in summer. No one believes one causes the other, yet many headlines run far looser cause-and-effect logic than that.

Figure 6. Confusing Correlation with Cause

DAILY POST

New Study Finds

SMARTPHONES CAUSE ANXIETY

Rates of anxiety rise alongside device adoption, researchers report

A recent study has revealed a significant correlation between smartphone usage and rising levels of anxiety. Researchers indicate that as smartphone ownership increases, rates of anxiety disorders

Who was studied, and how were they selected?
What else changed during the study period?
How was anxiety measured?
Does correlation really support the conclusion?

Bias adds another twist. Sometimes data is biased because it captures an unbalanced set of people, places, or circumstances. Sometimes the bias comes from who makes choices about what to measure and why. Sometimes the bias is in us, because we enjoy conclusions that match what we already believe.

Bias doesn't make data useless. It just means conclusions need a second look before they're trusted.

Confusing correlation with cause and blindly accepting bias are familiar paths to incorrect conclusions and bad outcomes.

Misleading numbers and visuals

Numbers and visuals can be technically correct and still deeply misleading. Common moves include:

- Shrinking or expanding axes to exaggerate change
- Cropping time windows to hide reversals or spikes
- Using percentages without showing counts
- Comparing groups that aren't actually comparable

Figure 7. Misleading Charts and Visual Distortion

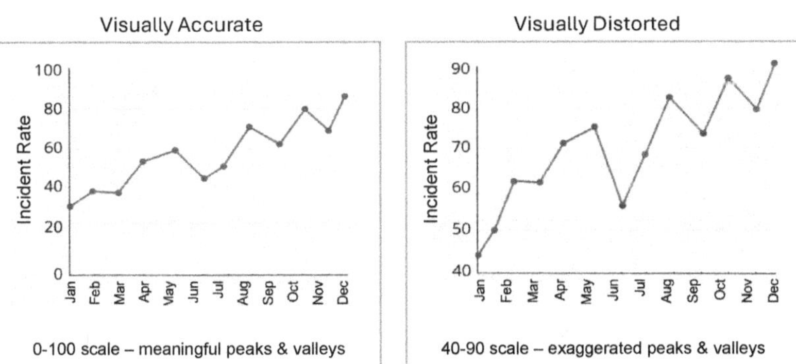

Charts are persuasive because they compress a lot of information into a small space. That compression has trade-offs. Titles, labels, and time ranges do quiet but essential work anchoring interpretation.

Here's a useful habit: if a chart feels dramatic, pause and ask what choices made it dramatic. Color, scaling, and selective comparisons can steer conclusions faster than a paragraph of text.

Visuals are powerful because they give the illusion of direct observation—if it's on a chart, it must be real. But numbers can misbehave in pictures just as easily as in words. A thoughtful viewer asks enough questions to understand the chart and its limits before letting it steer beliefs, decisions, or debates.

Ethics, rights, and power

When data influences decisions about people, ethics must be part of the conversation. Choices about measurement, classification, and reporting affect how opportunities, resources, and attention are distributed.

> *When data affects people and lives, questions about power and ethics should be asked.*

Questions worth asking include:

- Whose experiences are included, and whose are missing?
- How will this information be used, and what do people know about that use?
- Who benefits if the data is believed, and who bears the risk if it's wrong?
- What accountability exists when decisions cause harm?

Power matters because data often comes from institutions that can define terms, set standards, decide what counts, and determine what is visible. Data literacy includes being alert to these dynamics and recognizing that neutrality can never be assumed.

Habits of skepticism and careful thinking

Reasoning with data isn't heroic. It's practical and slow. Habits matter more than technical skill.

A few powerful habits include:

- Checking where a number came from before sharing it
- Comparing more than one source for important decisions
- Noticing what wasn't measured and who wasn't counted
- Asking what evidence would change your mind
- Revisiting outcomes to see if initial interpretations held up

The goal is informed trust: the kind that asks questions, listens for context, and keeps conclusions flexible enough to rethink when new information arrives. This sort of careful thinking is a good alternative to cynicism and mistrust.

Questioning and measured skepticism are healthy data literacy habits.

Questioning data isn't about being difficult. It's about being fair to the data, to the people affected by decisions, and to the complexity of the world the data attempts to describe.

FIVE

Decision Making with Data

Data matters most when it influences what people do. At some point, numbers stop being merely interesting and become actionable. They become part of choices about health, money, work, and civic life. Data rarely speaks alone: it complements *and* competes with memory, experience, obligations, values, budgets, deadlines, and instincts. Most decisions blend measurable inputs with experiences, beliefs, and values.

Data matters most when it influences what people do.

Data's role varies across settings. A parent deciding whether a child needs extra help draws on different information than a warehouse supervisor planning staff for the weekend and a voter judging the impact of a policy proposal. Yet the underlying questions often repeat: *Is this enough to move? What's at stake if I'm wrong? How confident do I need to be?*

Decision making also includes decisions about the data itself—how much to trust it, when to treat it as tentative, and how to learn from outcomes. Confidence is earned, not assumed, and feedback often teaches more than the initial decision did.

Personal and family decisions

Data shows up in family life in small but persistent ways. Growth charts, symptom logs, sleep trackers, appointment histories, billing summaries, calendars, and time-blocking apps all offer clues about how life is going. None of these tells the whole story, yet each contributes a piece.

Decisions here often revolve around simple questions: *Is this working? Is this safe? Can we afford this? Is this fair? Is this helping?*

Numbers are but one part of understanding and decision making. They are one voice in a conversation. A parent might look at a test score along with classroom work, stress level, and curiosity about the subject. An adult comparing a household budget to spending trends may decide that the real issue is weekends, holidays, subscriptions, or simply the need for clear priorities.

> *Data is one voice in a conversation, not the final word.*
> *Good decisions blend data with*
> *experience, values, and judgment.*

Many of the things that families care about, such as joy, confidence, friendship, belonging, and creativity, resist measurement. Data and numbers aren't good at reflecting the human factors in decision making.

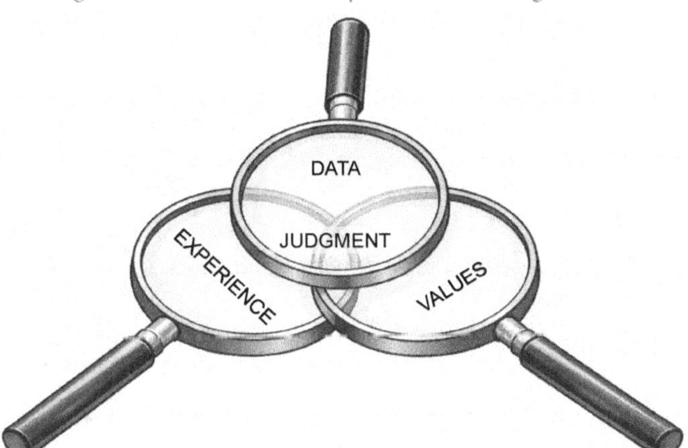

Figure 8. Personal and Family Decision-Making Lenses

Communication helps make choices visible. Sharing a chart of screen time, a simple savings tracker, or a color-coded chore board helps align expectations and reduce guesswork. When children participate in updating these records, they learn that data is something they can influence and understand, not just something that lands on them from the outside. That, in itself, is early data literacy.

Decision making at work

Workplaces depend on information to coordinate action. Decisions range from quick triage (*Which support tickets go first?*)

to longer-term choices about staffing, scheduling, investments, and priorities. Different roles see different forms of data, such as queue metrics, gauges, dashboards, spreadsheets, and forecasts. But the different roles and data forms often bring similar questions: *Is this information fit for what I'm trying to do? What action does it suggest? What are the risks of getting it wrong?*

Workplaces run on data and information—
and on the people who question it.

For frontline and operational roles, decision making is woven into the flow of tasks. Service staff juggle attention and escalation; logistics workers adapt to capacity constraints; compliance roles interpret policies in context. These decisions rely on what systems report and what conditions look like in real life. When inventory counts don't match what's on the shelves, or wait times feel longer than dashboards imply, workers reconcile differences, raise concerns, and adjust. Recording information accurately is part of this workflow because downstream decisions depend on upstream care.

Administrative and office roles involve coordinating, handling paperwork, meeting deadlines, and managing workload. Schedules, forms, handoffs, and backlog reports influence choices about timing, sequencing, and escalation. A missing approval, a conflicting record, or an ambiguous form can change the shape of a day. Communication is also a decision: what to send, to whom, and at what level of detail. Data helps these processes run smoothly, and when it doesn't, people improvise—another kind of judgment rooted in literacy.

Leadership, technical, and specialist roles use data to set targets, define success, manage risk, and evaluate impact. Choosing the right indicators is a responsibility, not a formality. So is recognizing when numbers create certainty that isn't real, such as when a model's confidence is high, but its data is narrow, biased, or outdated.

Confidence is earned, not assumed.
Knowing when NOT to trust a number is a data literacy skill.

Across roles, knowing when not to trust data is part of the skill set. Sudden jumps, shifting definitions, missing data, and mismatches with observation are signals to pause. Workplaces that encourage questions and corrections without blame make better use of data because they make it safer to point out when something is off.

Civic and community decisions

Civic life depends on shared information. Statistics about crime, employment, housing, education, health, and climate all feed into opinions, debates, policies, and ballot choices. Dashboards, charts, maps, and sound bites circulate through news, campaigns, and social platforms, helping people decide what issues matter and what should be done about them.

Data-literate participants ask grounding questions: *How is this measured? Who is included (and excluded)? What time period is shown? What uncertainty is acknowledged? What comparisons are implied?*

They look for independent sources and historical context, not just dramatic headlines.

Civic decisions aren't limited to elections. Communities decide how schools are run, how transportation works, how parks are funded, how public safety is approached, and how services are delivered. Participation can be quiet (forming an opinion), procedural (filling out a survey or voting), or active (showing up at meetings, organizing, advocating). In each case, information influences judgment.

Communities sometimes gather their own data, such as local surveys, mapping projects, observational counts, or shared stories that document conditions. These efforts reveal differences that summary statistics can hide, such as how air quality varies block by block or how transit reliability differs by time of day. Making variation visible is often the first step toward making change plausible.

Decisions about the data: evaluating and learning

Decision making with data includes evaluating the data itself. Information varies in relevance, completeness, timeliness, and quality. Sometimes the right choice is to act confidently. At other times, caution and questioning are good choices. Knowing the difference is a literacy skill.

Signals that information deserves skepticism include mismatched definitions, unexplained shifts in how something is counted, conflicts across credible sources, and gaps that exclude entire groups or regions. When uncertainty arises, people may seek clarification, cross-check against alternatives, discount the weight of the information, or delay a decision until more context emerges. Automated systems that assign scores or classifications introduce new wrinkles: when data outputs conflict with judgment or experience, it is reasonable to question the system rather than defer to it.

Decision making includes decisions about the data itself.

Evaluation also includes learning from outcomes. After a decision, it helps to ask: *What information was used, and why? What was missing or hard to measure? Did the outcome match expectations? If not, what might explain the difference?*

These reflections strengthen intuition about how much evidence is enough for different decisions and which questions are worth asking before acting.

---

*Data rarely eliminates uncertainty—
it helps people to navigate it.*

The goal is steady improvement—using information thoughtfully, transparently, and in alignment with values. The aim is not perfection. Data does not eliminate uncertainty or make decisions easy.

Six

Communicating with Data

Data turns into influence once it is communicated. When people make sense of what the data shows and why it matters, the next step is to help others see it too. That process turns private understanding into shared understanding. This leads to decisions made together instead of in isolation.

> *Communication is how understanding spreads from individuals to groups.*

Communicating with data involves deciding what information to include, how to present it, and how to engage with questions that follow. The message may be visual, verbal, written, or a mix; the right form depends on the audience and what they need to be able to understand and act.

Communication works best as conversation. Others bring context, concerns, and ideas the communicator can't foresee.

They may reinforce the message, add nuance, and challenge the logic. Good communication invites this exchange because it strengthens both understanding and decisions.

Communication is one of the most human parts of data literacy. It asks for clarity, empathy, and curiosity: skills that shape how families plan, how workplaces coordinate, and how communities make choices together.

Creating and selecting data

Communication begins with choices about what data to include. Sometimes that means creating data: tracking steps, noting symptoms, logging expenses, or tallying how often something happens. Other times it means selecting from data that already exists: numbers from a dashboard, summaries from a report, records from a system or database.

Selection is intentional—
choosing data that helps to share understanding.

Selection is guided by purpose. A parent chooses both test scores and reading logs to discuss progress. A worker chooses queue lengths and staffing levels to explain delays. A community group chooses enrollment counts, transit frequency, and housing prices to show how a neighborhood is changing. The data is chosen not because it is available, but because it helps others understand the situation at hand.

From data to message

Turning data into a message starts with purpose. *Who needs to understand this? What are they deciding or doing? And what response or action should the message support?*

Audience matters. A family member may need only the bottom line ("expenses are trending up"), while a colleague may need details to adjust a plan. A community meeting may need context before numbers make sense. Messages can inform, motivate, clarify, validate, or prompt a choice.

Context matters too. People bring expectations, assumptions, and prior knowledge. Communicating with data means meeting them where they are—choosing relatable examples, defining unfamiliar terms, and connecting the message to what they already know.

---

*The right message depends on
purpose, audience, and context.*

Once the audience and purpose are clear, the message takes shape. It may highlight a change ("screen time has increased this month"), a pattern ("weekend spending runs higher than weekdays"), a comparison ("attendance matches last year"), or variation ("store performance ranges widely"). Each of these suggests meaning and invites others to ask questions or consider actions.

Figure 9. Crafting the Message

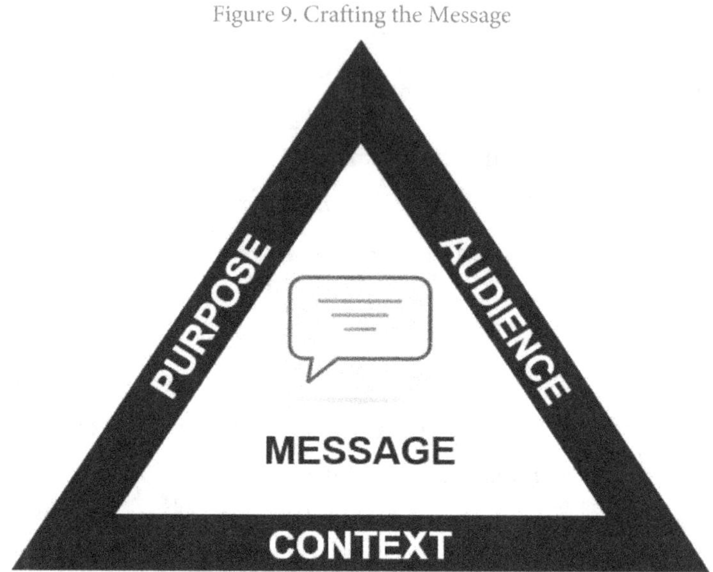

Choosing how to deliver the message—visually, verbally, in writing, or some combination—is part of the craft. Visuals make patterns and relationships easy to see; narrative describes reasoning, conclusions, limits, and sometimes recommendations. The right form is the one that best connects with the audience.

Framing carries responsibility. Overlooking uncertainty, cherry-picking comparisons, or presenting rare cases as typical can distort understanding. The balance to aim for is clarity with honesty: clear enough to be understood, and honest enough not to overstate confidence or precision.

Communicating visually

Visuals help people grasp structure, scale, and change quickly. Charts, diagrams, timelines, and maps turn patterns into something the eye can follow. A line chart can show a trend in seconds; a bar chart can compare categories with little effort.

Effective visuals begin with clarity about the message. Titles, labels, scales, and time ranges anchor interpretation. Color guides attention, but it can also overstate differences or imply importance where none exists. Visual form matters as well: lines suggest continuity, bars emphasize comparison, scatter plots show relationships, and maps reveal spatial variation.

Visuals highlight patterns.
They reveal structure, scale,
and change faster than words.

Visuals can mislead if design choices do the talking instead of the data. Cropping, scaling, selective time windows, or dramatic styling can make small effects look large or large effects look trivial. When visuals are honest, they help others see what the data shows and what it doesn't.

Viewing visuals is its own skill. A careful reader checks what is being measured, over what period, and against what comparison. They ask whether groups are similar, whether definitions match, and whether the numbers are exact, approximate, or estimated. A brief pause to examine the basics prevents the framing from steering the conclusion on its own.

Communicating with words

Not every message needs a chart. Words carry nuance, tone, and reasoning that numbers alone can't express. They explain what the data means in a particular situation and why it matters.

Words can stand alone or complement visuals. Spoken communication shapes family decisions, classroom instruction, healthcare, and civic meetings. Written communication appears in reports, updates, digital media, and workplace decision-making processes. The form changes, but the job is the same: connect information to the choices people face.

Words explain meaning.
They add nuance, tone,
and human factors not apparent in visuals.

Words can explain relationships ("shipments are delayed because orders doubled"), make comparisons ("this winter is warmer than usual"), express uncertainty ("we're not sure if this increase will continue"), or provide context. They help with the parts of decisions that are hard to measure: convenience, safety, values, fairness, and trade-offs.

Stories are particularly useful when the goal is understanding. A story introduces a question, presents relevant information, and links it to consequences and choices. Effective data storytelling makes meaning easy to understand and to follow. Stories are sticky. People remember them, repeat them, and share them, making them a natural way for insights to travel.

Figure 10. Storytelling with Data

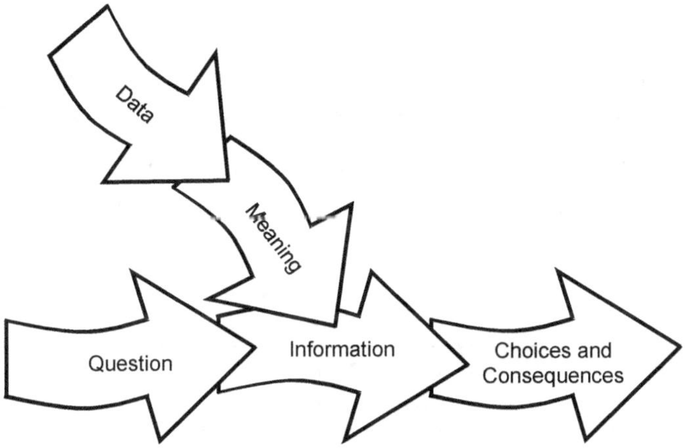

Words also bring in the human elements that sit alongside data. Feelings, constraints, expectations, and values shape how people interpret information and how they decide what to do. A budget discussion that includes both spending patterns and stress levels gives a fuller picture than either one alone.

Dialog, feedback, and listening

Presenting data is only the beginning of conversations. Once numbers, visuals, and explanations are shared, others respond.

They compare, question, add context, and connect information to what they already know.

Feedback takes many forms. Clarifying questions surface missing context. Supportive comments validate patterns that match lived experience. Challenges and alternative explanations widen the search for meaning. Feedback can strengthen confidence or reveal blind spots—both are useful.

Listening matters on both sides. Those sharing information need to hear how it was understood and where confusion lingers. Those receiving information need to listen for the reasoning, intent, and limitations behind the message. When everyone listens, shared understanding grows.

Good communication is not a broadcast—
it is a conversation.

Good communication with data often unfolds in loops. A message is refined, a chart clarified, a comparison adjusted, or an assumption made explicit. Through iteration, communication becomes a process that improves ideas, sharpens decisions, and builds collective understanding.

Data Literacy Across Roles and Life

Data doesn't show up the same way for everyone. A growth chart at a pediatric check-up, a queue dashboard at work, a test score sent home from school, a headline about jobs, a budget spreadsheet, a city map, a credit score, a performance review. Each belongs to a different corner of life and asks people to make sense of information in different ways.

This part of the book examines data literacy from those varied vantage points. It begins with children and students, moves through families and participation in public life, then into work in its many forms, and finally to people who shape decisions in organizations and public life.

Data and data literacy look different depending on where you're looking from.
Data plays many roles because people play many roles.

Each chapter describes what data looks like from a particular point of view, what habits and skills matter most in that setting, and where responsibilities and risks commonly appear. It also discusses how decisions made in one setting may ripple into others: how family choices influence schools, how workplace policies affect communities, and how civic decisions shape everyday life.

Together, these perspectives show data literacy as part of how people learn, decide, and act as they move through life stages and fill multiple roles in daily life.

SEVEN

Growing Up with Data: Children and Students

Young children meet data long before they hear the word. Sticker charts, weather wheels, counting games, and attendance tallies turn everyday happenings into marks that can be compared and talked about. A preschooler might proudly announce, "We had more sunny days than rainy days!" This is a small but meaningful act of data sense-making.

Figure 11. From Counting to Questioning: How Data Habits Grow

At this age, literacy is built through ordinary experiences:

- Counting people in line or days until a birthday
- Comparing who has more blocks and whether that feels fair
- Sorting objects by color or size
- Tracking progress toward a shared goal using stickers or tally marks

These activities teach that information can be recorded, added up, and revisited to answer familiar questions, like *How many? Or Which happened more?* Numbers become more than math problems. They are seen as ways of describing what is happening in the world around us.

Children also learn that numbers can be wrong or incomplete. One child notices a missing weather sticker and asks to recount. Another insists the turn-taking tally is off. In these moments, they are questioning data and defending fairness, skills that matter throughout life wherever data is encountered.

---

*Questioning the numbers is often
the first sign of critical thinking.*

Early lessons in safety and privacy can be woven in gently. Adults explain which information is fine to share (first names, favorite colors) and which should stay private (addresses, passwords). Simple rules like "Ask before sharing photos" and "We don't tell strangers where we live" connect data to concrete safety habits children can understand.

> *Data skills should be part of early education.*
> *Just as reading and writing begin in elementary school,*
> *the habits of data literacy can begin there as well.*

In these early years, the goals are familiarity and confidence. Data is part of games, routines, and stories. Questions like *Is this right?* and *Is this fair?* are normal parts of conversation. Data skills should be part of early education. Just as reading and writing begin in elementary school, the habits of data literacy can begin there as well. Skills with formal data tools and techniques come later in life.

Students and youth: habits that last

As children move into the school years, they encounter more formal data and more digital data. Grades, test scores, attendance records, feedback rubrics, and learning dashboards come into play. These signals matter, not because students need to become analysts, but because they build lasting habits for interpreting information.

School offers structured opportunities to practice:

- **Designing small projects**: Collecting simple data and charting it.
- **Checking for errors**: Asking why a vote has more votes than voters.
- **Interpreting visuals**: Spotting trends instead of reciting exact values.

Projects tied to real life, such as sleep patterns, homework time, reading habits, screen time, show how data connects to everyday choices and to the real world. Students see that evidence can support or challenge intuition, and that they can generate their own evidence.

Metrics and indicators are not conclusions. They're clues.

Digital platforms add another layer. Apps track streaks, badges, completion percentages, and "time spent." These metrics feel personal, but they don't always mean what they seem. A login streak might indicate steady practice, or it might indicate opening an app for ten seconds to keep the streak alive. Completion badges indicate finishing a sequence, not long-term understanding. Discussing these distinctions helps students see metrics as indicators, not as conclusions.

Privacy and consent become more complex as platforms collect data by default. Students encounter permission forms, settings menus, and terms of service that they rarely read. Guided conversation can surface real questions:

- What information is being collected?
- Who can see it, and for how long?
- If the data is widely shared, who will be affected, and how?

These conversations help young people understand that they can make choices about data. Their influence doesn't look the same in every situation. Sometimes they choose, sometimes they push back, sometimes they ask, and sometimes they simply notice and adjust. What matters is learning that data can be discussed, clarified, questioned, challenged, and shaped.

Critical literacy for youth

Adolescence is a turning point for the development of critical habits. Teens encounter claims, statistics, and visuals in news, social media, advertising, and school assignments, often without clear guidance on how to evaluate them. Learning to think with and about data is as important as learning to work with the numbers.

Practical skills include:

- **Questioning sources**: Who made this number or chart, and why?
- **Checking scope**: How many people or events does this describe?
- **Looking for what's missing**: Which groups, time periods, or outcomes are not shown?
- **Spotting visual tricks**: Distorted axes, cropped time windows, emotional color choices.

Skepticism isn't cynicism.
It is curiosity coupled with questions.

Students can practice on real examples: campaign ads, product rankings, influencer claims, and viral charts. Comparing multiple sources reveals that disagreement is normal and informative.

Youth also begin using data to make everyday decisions: how to manage limited money, how much time to spend studying, and which opportunities to pursue. Tracking small bits of information like sleep, spending, and practice time helps them test assumptions and adjust their plans when reality doesn't match expectations.

Ethics enter the picture, too. Teens notice when systems label schools, neighborhoods, and people. They ask whether rules feel fair, whether online tools reinforce stereotypes, and who gains when information mostly flows toward companies or institutions. These conversations do not need everyone to agree; they just need space so curiosity, questioning, and care feel like normal reactions to data.

Supporting young people's literacy

Children and students learn data literacy through observation. They learn it in relationships with parents, caregivers, teachers, and peers. Adults don't need technical expertise to help. Demonstrating curiosity, caution, and reflection goes a long way toward illustrating data literacy habits.

Helpful practices include:

- **Thinking aloud**: *This chart shows progress, but only for the last few weeks—what else do we know?*

- **Inviting questions**: Encouraging kids to ask *How do you know?* or *Is that fair?*

- **Routine error-checking**: Treating recounting and corrections as responsible, not embarrassing.

- **Sharing decisions**: Using simple visuals for family schedules, budgets, or goals, and asking what children notice.

Schools can integrate data literacy across subjects. History shows that numbers have been used as evidence to argue for change, defend decisions, and shape public opinion. Science helps students practice collecting observations, comparing results, and talking about uncertainty—not everything has a single right answer. Arts and media highlight how visuals affect interpretation. That is, how color, framing, and emphasis can make information persuasive, confusing, or compelling.

Libraries, youth programs, and community groups can help young people explore local issues by using evidence, such as mapping playground access, charting bus frequency, or conducting surveys about after-school activities. These experiences show that communities can tell their own stories with data.

Data habits built in childhood don't disappear.
They grow and mature.

Across childhood and adolescence, we can actively foster confident, curious, and thoughtful data users. We can cultivate young people who can understand information, ask good questions, and use what they learn in everyday life and later in adulthood.

EIGHT

Data in Personal and Community Life

Most interaction with data happens outside offices and classrooms. It shows up in households, stores and apps, neighborhood conversations, and the steady flow of news and services that surround daily life. These contexts rarely announce themselves as "data work," yet they ask people to interpret information, question claims, make decisions, and sometimes advocate for themselves or for others.

Figure 12. Data In Every Aspect of Life

The roles here are ordinary, such as parent, caregiver, shopper, patient, learner, neighbor, voter, volunteer, and participant. The activities are ordinary too: choosing a product, interpreting a school or clinic dashboard, reading a headline, comparing offers, or filling out a form. Everyday life is full of these small data encounters. Together, they form a quiet but significant layer of data literacy, shaping how people understand what's happening and what to do next.

Data shows up in everyday life—
often not recognized as such.

Parenting and caregiving

Parents and caregivers work with information constantly, even when they don't consciously recognize it as data. Growth charts, immunization records, symptom logs, school portals, billing summaries, sleep trackers, calendars, and medication schedules combine to build partial views of children, elders, and others in their care. None of these things tells the whole story; each offers one window into well-being, progress, or need.

Interpretation matters. A borderline test result might be alarming until a doctor provides context about ranges and variation. An attendance dashboard might look worrisome without noting that a flu wave hit the entire classroom. A learning platform's "engagement score" may reflect clicks or logins with no information about the depth of attention. Literate caregivers weigh multiple sources of evidence, such as professional judgment, observation, personal history, and patterns over time, before reaching conclusions.

Caregiving increasingly includes digital life. Apps for children and elders track sleep, steps, "productive minutes," and streaks. These metrics feel personal, but don't always mean what they seem. A reading streak might reflect genuine practice, or just a habit of opening an app briefly to avoid losing progress. "Time spent" may include idle minutes when the device sat open on the table. People often discuss what these numbers measure, what they encourage, and how they align with values such as independence, responsibility, respect, safety, or rest.

Privacy and consent decisions also arise at home. Parents decide when to enable location tracking, whether to share photos, which apps are acceptable, and how long data should linger in cloud backups. Many of these choices balance convenience, protection, and autonomy. These are practical considerations, not technical issues. Privacy and consent involve asking what information is collected, who sees it, how long it lasts, and how it might shape behavior.

Caregiving uses information, intuition,
and empathy together.

Caregiving is emotionally-charged work. Data does not replace intuition, empathy, or care. It supports them sometimes by confirming concern, sometimes by offering reassurance, and sometimes by signaling that a conversation or a second opinion is needed.

Choosing and using products, platforms, and services

As consumers, people encounter data when comparing prices, selecting services, and evaluating digital products. Bills, terms, ratings, reviews, risk scores, and usage summaries all hint at how choices will play out over time. The challenge today is the abundance of information—sorting through what's relevant, reliable, trustworthy, and useful.

Comparison often starts with top-line numbers such as monthly cost, discount percentage, interest rate, fee, deductible, and usage limit. But these figures rarely stand alone. A "low price" may pair with steep fees. A "savings estimate" may assume perfect discipline that no one actually maintains. A "data cap" or "number of streams" may matter more than the sticker price for how a service is experienced.

Digital platforms introduce persuasion to the mix. Recommendations, rankings, and personalized offers use past behavior to predict future preferences. Sometimes this is helpful by surfacing options someone might not have found otherwise. Sometimes it produces a narrowing effect by showing only what the system expects based on a few early clicks. Here, literacy involves recognizing personalization as a form of argument: "You might like this" is a suggestion, not a certainty.

Data also allows people to advocate for themselves. When disputes arise over billing, service quality, repairs, or delivery, simple records make a difference. Dates, screenshots, amounts, and prior contacts clarify what happened and reduce friction. Over time, this habit reinforces the idea that keeping small records is good practice. It is not bureaucracy; it is self-protection and self-advocacy.

Evaluating advice and claims

Advice aimed at households can be unrelenting, especially in areas such as health, finances, parenting, nutrition, fitness, and supplements. Nearly all of it arrives with some kind of data. Sometimes the data is numbers dressed up as evidence, such as success rates, averages, and percentages. Sometimes the data is narrative like stories, testimonials, and promises designed to persuade. Some of that data is well-grounded. Much of it relies on limited evidence, selective examples, and unsupported claims.

Data literacy helps people pose quiet questions that reveal the strength of a claim:

- What does "success" mean in this context?

- How many people were involved in a study, and how similar are they to my situation?
- What's being counted, and what is *not* being counted?
- Are side effects, trade-offs, or uncertainties described?
- Who benefits if this claim is taken at face value?

Curiosity is a great form of protection.

These questions aren't technical. They're curiosity in action. For many families, emotional context matters as much as evidence. Worry or hope can make any statistic more persuasive. Pausing to check multiple sources, consult a trusted professional, or compare definitions reduces the pull of sensational claims.

Similar skills apply to consumer persuasion. Reviews, ratings, and rankings can shape what people choose to buy, but they don't all tell the same story. For example, a product with an average rating of 4.7 stars sounds impressive, but that single number leaves out important details. A simple chart showing how many people gave each rating can reveal much more—such as whether most people rated it highly or if opinions are split between very high and very low scores. A testimonial tells even less without context about typical results. Numbers can summarize experience at scale, but without understanding how they were collected, it is hard to know what they really reflect.

Navigating public information

Public information, such as headlines, dashboards, charts, maps, and official notices, shapes how people understand communities and world events. The topics vary: jobs, health, housing, safety, climate, education, transportation, budgets, or elections. Interpretation hinges on context: definitions, time spans, categories, baselines, and groups included.

A graph showing change over time may look dramatic if the vertical axis is cropped or if the time window is short. A ranking of "best places to live" may hide the weighting factors used for factors such as affordability, safety, and amenities. A statistic about crime rates or graduation rates may depend on specific counting rules that exclude groups not captured in administrative systems. None of this requires cynicism, but rather only a pause to ask what is being measured and what comparisons are implied.

Context turns information into understanding.

Reliable public understanding rarely comes from a single source. Checking a second source, especially one with a different audience or mission, often clarifies ambiguity and corrects exaggeration. Over time, people build an instinct for which outlets chase drama, which supply context, and which value transparency.

Participating in community

Participation takes many forms: answering surveys, attending meetings, researching ballot measures, advocating for local issues, volunteering, and contributing to community groups. In each case, information becomes a basis for conversation and decision making.

Community data can be formal (official statistics) or informal (neighbors comparing notes). Sometimes communities collect data for themselves, such as mapping playground access, tracking bus frequency, surveying renters about maintenance, and recording air quality block by block. These efforts make variation visible and highlight gaps not apparent in aggregated statistics.

Participation also involves contributing data. Filling out a census, responding to a school survey, and sharing information with a community project can all improve representation and decision making. Data contribution carries risk, so literate participants weigh privacy and purpose: *Why is this being asked? Who will use it? What safeguards exist? What benefits might come from more active participation?*

The goal is to make participation feel possible and worthwhile. When information is openly discussed, compared, and questioned, decisions become easier to understand, even when people disagree about what should be done.

Bringing it together

Across activities such as caregiving, choosing services, evaluating claims, making purchases, interpreting news, and participating in the community, data literacy shifts from something abstract to something experienced every day. It shows up in budgeting conversations, school meetings, medical appointments, household debates, neighborhood chats, and civic decisions. Data literacy in everyday life is shaped by curiosity, judgment, interpretation, and shared understanding.

Families and communities use information to make choices, set priorities, and take action. They question, compare, adapt, and sometimes advocate. These habits deepen over time and prepare people for the data encounters they encounter at work and in public life.

NINE

Data in Work and Public Life

Work in all its forms runs on information. Requests, records, schedules, tickets, forms, logs, notes, dashboards, and reports help people understand what has happened, what is happening, and what needs to happen next. These records support day-to-day work: organizing tasks, coordinating handoffs, maintaining safety and quality, meeting obligations, communicating with colleagues, and explaining decisions when questions arise.

Workers intuitively know when they're working with data. They rely on information to adjust to changing conditions, solve problems, raise questions, and advocate for changing practices. Data literacy in this setting spans understanding, interpretation, judgment, questioning, analysis, communication, and decision making—skills that make shared work possible.

Data moves through the workplace. Data recorded by one worker will travel through workgroups, processes, and systems, affecting downstream processes such as scheduling, billing, automation, safety checks, quality controls, customer interactions, and institutional reporting.

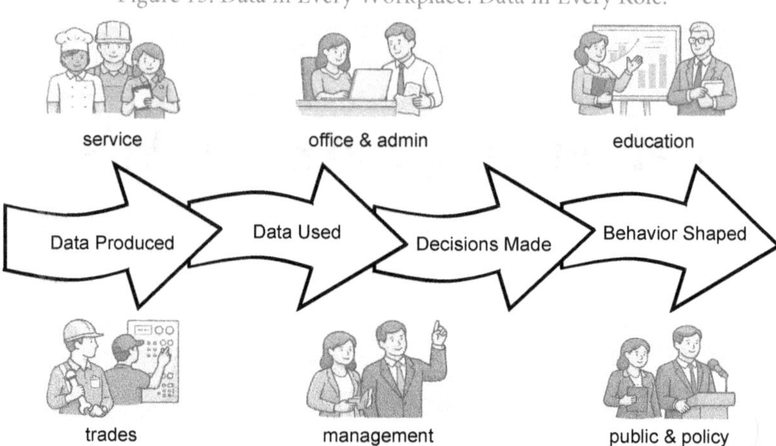

Figure 13. Data in Every Workplace. Data in Every Role.

Know where the data that you use is produced.
Know where the data that you produce is used.

Understanding how information flows through the workplace helps workers to see why accuracy, clarity, timeliness, and classification matter. Small choices, such as how something is labeled, when updates are made, and how much detail is included, shape how data is understood and how decisions are made downstream.

Service workers

Service work spans many settings, including retail, hospitality, transportation, recreation, call centers, healthcare support, and personal services. Across these environments, people work with a mix of records, tickets, schedules, notes, forms, reservations, requests, and feedback. These items provide important information such as what customers need, what has been done, and what remains in the queue.

Systems used in service rely on information such as:

- **Counts**: Calls waiting, orders in progress, tables open, rooms occupied.
- **Timings**: Wait time, service time, turnaround time.
- **Statuses**: Open/closed tickets, assigned/unassigned cases, in-progress tasks.
- **Feedback**: Surveys, comments, reviews, star ratings.

These kinds of data guide prioritization and coordination. A long queue might reflect heavy demand, short staffing, or complex cases. A low rating might reflect frustration with a policy, dissatisfaction with service, or issues beyond the worker's control. Interpreting data in context helps uncover causes and choose appropriate actions.

Workers compare what systems report with what they observe. If a dashboard shows "no calls waiting" while people remain on hold, or if reservations show open tables even though the dining room is full, something is misaligned. Treating mismatches as cues for escalation or clarification supports smooth operations and fair decisions.

Accurate record keeping is a form of quiet data work. Tagging tickets, updating reservations, and noting completion times will influence downstream activities such as billing, staffing, capacity planning, and performance reviews. These updates contribute to organizational memory: what happened, when, and under what conditions.

Simple record keeping often has big consequences.

Service roles involve sensitive customer information: payment details, contact information, identity documents, loyalty profiles, and sometimes medical or dietary details. Data literacy here includes ethical and compliant handling of information: understanding confidentiality expectations, access limits, retention rules, and regulatory obligations. It also involves recognizing how privacy, safety, and trust work together in customer-facing environments.

Trade workers and technicians

Trades and technical workers, such as technicians, mechanics, construction workers, manufacturing operators, utilities staff, and many others, work close to physical systems. In addition to tools, machines, and materials, they also work with information:

measurements, diagrams, specifications, checklists, logs, and alarms that describe how equipment and processes behave over time.

They work with data such as:

- Gauges, readouts, tolerances, and thresholds
- Defect logs, maintenance histories, and inspection reports
- Blueprints, CAD drawings, building plans, and specifications
- Permits, site conditions, schedules, and change orders
- Digital sensors, alarms, automation controls, and equipment logs
- Safety checklists, certifications, and work orders

Data literacy in these settings includes interpreting ranges, variation, and tolerance. A small temperature rise may be harmless in one system and dangerous in another. A one-inch deviation on a plan may be trivial in one trade and unacceptable in another. Knowing when a value signals normal variation, drift, failure, or rework is central to both safety and continuity.

Technical work also relies on calibration and verification. Instruments must be checked to be sure that the measurements they provide are consistently reliable. Weather and site conditions add noise to measurements in construction. Literate workers understand that automation and scheduling systems can only act on what they detect; miscalibration or missing context can produce both false alarms and silent failures.

Cross-checking data against direct observation is a daily habit. Workers question readings that seem implausible ("pump off but showing high pressure" or "plans show clearance for ductwork, but field measurement shows the beam sits lower") and may remeasure, request recalibration, or document anomalies with photos. These small acts of skepticism prevent misinterpretation and support root-cause analysis when problems arise.

Testing data against reality is a form of
data quality assurance.

Documentation (what was done, when, by whom, and under what conditions) supports preventive maintenance, scheduling, warranty decisions, inspections, and regulatory compliance. For construction, documentation provides evidence for sequencing, site conditions, change orders, and handoffs across subcontractors. These records protect workers, reduce disputes, and improve systems.

Trades and technical workers frequently encounter sensitive data. Safety incidents, medical clearances, identity and certification data, access control logs, and many kinds of environment and event data must be handled responsibly. Data literacy includes ethical and compliant handling of information: understanding which data is confidential, how long it should be retained, who can access it, and how privacy, safety, and trust are supported.

Finally, ethics and fairness shape how operational data is used. Logs, defect reports, and incident records can be tools for blame or tools for improvement. Cultures that encourage honest reporting without punishment elevate safety, reliability, and resilience of systems, and ultimately protect both workers and the public.

Office and administrative workers

Office and administrative workers, including administrative assistants, coordinators, schedulers, HR support, billing and claims staff, and intake roles, keep information and coordination flowing across organizations. Their work blends records, communication, decision support, and follow-through. This work depends heavily on data.

Office and administrative workers encounter many kinds of information, including:

- Schedules and calendars
- Contact lists and routing information
- Forms and case files
- Invoices, purchase orders, and billing records
- Correspondence and meeting notes
- Records, summaries, and audit trails

Some of this information is structured; some is narrative or descriptive. Some is quantitative (numbers that measure things) and some is qualitative (describing characteristics of things or assigning categories to things). All of it influences how tasks are assigned, how questions are resolved, and how work moves across departments and systems. And all of it requires data literacy skills.

Reconciling and maintaining records are essential skills in these roles. Matching names, dates, identifiers, amounts, and other data across systems prevents confusion, rework, and delays. This is core data quality work (even if not formally recognized as such) because accuracy and completeness of data at the front of a process affect everything that follows.

Data quality is a core responsibility in the workplace.

Routing and escalating information is a routine part of data work in these roles. Office and administrative workers act as connectors: they need to know who needs which information, when they need it, and in what form. This involves data consumption (reading and interpreting records), data creation (documenting and updating), and judgment (flagging anomalies or exceptions). Clear routing keeps work moving and supports decision making. When information reaches the right people in the right order, tasks flow, problems surface early, and mistakes don't pile up unnoticed.

Communicating with data and context is a visible part of office and administrative work. Status updates, scheduling notes, and routine correspondence often mix numbers with narrative. Providing the right amount of detail, neither too sparse nor overwhelming, helps colleagues understand circumstances and take the next steps. This form of communication supports shared decision making and reduces friction across teams.

The three skills of maintaining records, routing information, and communicating with data work together. Office and administrative roles sit at the intersection of data creation and data use: they collect information from others, document events as they happen, and update records that later inform decisions made by supervisors, analysts, leaders, regulators, and others. In many workplaces, these roles provide the connective tissue that keeps information coherent as it moves across people, systems, and time.

Privacy and confidentiality are everyday considerations. These roles frequently handle personal details, employment records, financial accounts, health information, internal correspondence, and other sensitive data. The volume and sensitivity of information are often greater here than in many other roles due to the breadth and variety of information involved. This makes careful data handling a core responsibility.

Data privacy and protection are fundamental responsibilities.

Data literacy in these roles includes knowing which information is sensitive—whether protected by law, governed by regulation, subject to contract compliance, or restricted by internal policy— and adjusting handling accordingly. Putting awareness into practice involves controlled access, secure storage, and appropriate retention and disposal. Protection against misrouted attachments, casual forwarding, and unsecured digital and physical files is important because these kinds of errors can expose people, violate policy, and erode trust.

Managers and leaders

Managers and leaders such as shift supervisors, team leads, department heads, program managers, and executives work at the junction of information and decision. Their responsibilities span planning, prioritizing, coordinating, resourcing, communicating, and evaluating. As the scope increases from small teams to large organizations, decisions ripple further and involve more people, more trade-offs, and greater uncertainty.

They work with many kinds of information:
- Performance and operations reports
- Staffing and scheduling information
- Budgets and financial summaries
- Risk, compliance, and policy requirements
- Customer, student, patient, or community feedback
- Forecasts, plans, and projections
- Dashboards and model outputs when using analytics, forecasting, or decision automation

Data literacy in this context blends interpretation, judgment, questioning, and clear communication. Managers use information to understand what is working, what needs attention, and where support or change might be needed. Leaders use it to compare options, consider trade-offs, and frame questions that shape how issues are understood inside the organization.

Managers and leaders are both consumers and producers of data. Their assessments, decisions, updates, and plans serve as information others rely on to guide schedules, budgets, initiatives, follow-up actions, compliance filings, and reporting. Choices about what to measure, how to define success, which comparisons matter, and which time horizons to consider create downstream obligations for colleagues and systems. Decisions about what to measure, how to classify work, and what to share internally or externally have ethical and cultural impacts.

Communication with data is a critical habit in these roles. Turning information into shared understanding allows strategy to translate into practice and practice to feed back into strategy. When managers and leaders communicate what is known, what remains uncertain, and what values guide decisions, they help colleagues align their efforts and make sense of direction, constraints, and priorities.

Data in managerial and leadership settings is rarely neutral. It carries privacy expectations, competitive sensitivities, and ethical considerations, especially when information affects employees, customers, students, patients, or the public. Managers and leaders set the tone for how sensitive information is handled: what is shared, with whom, and for what purpose.

Culture is shaped at this level. When leaders model curiosity, clarity, and fairness—asking whether measures reflect reality, whether comparisons are meaningful, and whether people are treated with respect—others follow suit. When managers pause to consider who is affected by a decision, how uncertainty should be communicated, or when consent is needed, they translate literacy into everyday ethics.

Measure the things that really matter.
Understand that measurement shapes
behavior and culture.

Good data habits scale. They influence how an organization thinks about privacy, confidentiality, transparency, and accountability. Over time, these habits become part of the shared culture: people feel safe asking questions, raising concerns, correcting errors, and contributing ideas. In this way, data literacy is more than a technical skill for managers and leaders; it is a practical responsibility for shaping how information is used and trusted across the organization.

Educators and education leaders

Educators include teachers, counselors, social workers, special-education staff, academic advisors, librarians, and others who work directly with learners. Education leaders include principals, department chairs, deans, district administrators, and superintendents. These are roles where decisions scale from classrooms to schools and districts. Together, they navigate information that spans student support, institutional operations, and community expectations.

Educators work with information that reflects individual learners and classroom contexts. Common examples include:

- Assessment results and growth measures
- Attendance, participation, and behavior records
- Learning plans and accommodations
- Coursework and portfolios
- Feedback from students and families
- Notes from counselors or support staff

These sources offer clues about strengths, needs, and progress, but they never capture a whole person. Data literacy for educators involves interpreting numbers in context; comparing present patterns with prior history; integrating information from multiple sources; balancing data with observation; avoiding deficit narratives; and questioning assumptions that attribute differences to individuals without considering resources or opportunity. These skills help educators support learners without reducing them to scores or dashboards.

Educators also help students build data literacy as a life skill. History shows how numbers shape public perceptions. Science emphasizes evidence, variation, and uncertainty. Mathematics builds comfort with quantities and graphs. Media and arts explore how visuals persuade. When data is framed as a tool for inquiry, students learn that they have roles and influence to determine how information is interpreted.

Education leaders encounter information on a broader scale than is typical for many other roles. Common educator data sources include:

- Enrollment trends and demographic data
- Staffing and scheduling information
- Budget and resource reports
- Program participation and completion rates
- Survey results from students, families, or staff
- Policy requirements, benchmarks, and compliance indicators

Data literacy for leaders involves a different but complementary set of skills: forming useful questions before looking at numbers; probing assumptions and definitions behind indicators; distinguishing signal from noise; weighing trade-offs across time horizons; integrating data with values and mission; and communicating evidence transparently to varied audiences. Leaders translate complex institutional information into guidance, priorities, and decisions that affect classrooms and communities.

Both educators and leaders work with sensitive information. Schools hold records that may involve disability status, medical needs, immigration status, disciplinary histories, family circumstances, or protected identity data. Literacy includes recognizing sensitivity; understanding access rules, retention requirements, and confidentiality expectations; and practicing careful handling in everyday work. External regulations matter, but so do internal policies about sharing, emailing, cloud storage, and access permissions.

Culture shapes how data is used. Leadership shapes whether information is used to support learning, highlight growth, and encourage collaboration, rather than for oversight and fault-finding. When educators and leaders model curiosity, fairness, and transparency—acknowledging uncertainty, welcoming questions, and using data to help instead of judge—they strengthen trust and demonstrate that data can support both people and institutions.

Public officials and policymakers

Public officials and policymakers, such as city council members, county supervisors, mayors, agency directors, legislative staff, and regulators, use population-level data to design and justify regulations, policies, budgets, and services. Their choices influence schools, transportation, health systems, environmental quality, land use, economic conditions, and much more.

They encounter a wide range of public data, including:

- Economic indicators (employment, inflation, wages, investment)
- Education metrics (graduation rates, test results, enrollment patterns)
- Health and environmental data (disease incidence, air quality, water levels, heat risk)
- Transportation and infrastructure statistics (traffic, transit usage, energy consumption)
- Demographic and housing data (migration, affordability, population change)
- Survey and polling results (public opinion, satisfaction, priorities)
- Forecasts and scenario models (climate, revenue, capacity, demand)

Data literacy in these roles spans several kinds of reasoning: questioning how indicators are defined, examining which groups are represented and which are missing, asking how long-term trends differ from short-term fluctuations, and understanding how uncertainty is handled in models and projections. Successful officials balance quantitative reasoning with qualitative knowledge from communities, frontline workers, and subject-matter experts.

Communication is central. Officials need to explain the evidence and trade-offs in ways that help people understand the decisions made and why they are made. Clear framing, accessible visuals, and honest discussion of limits and uncertainty strengthen trust; oversimplification or selective framing undermines it.

Public roles also rely on feedback loops that extend beyond data systems. Frontline workers, community organizations, and residents surface mismatches between policy intent and real-world outcomes—uneven effects across neighborhoods, unintended burdens on specific groups, or gaps unmeasured by official statistics. Listening to this feedback is part of responsible governance.

Sensitivity and rights considerations are significant in public settings. Many datasets involve identifiable individuals or vulnerable communities. Data literacy includes understanding legal and policy constraints on collection, retention, sharing, and linkage; assessing when data use may have risks; and recognizing that consent norms differ between mandatory and voluntary participation.

Public officials are both consumers and stewards of data. They decide what becomes public, what remains internal, how information is explained, and how people can appeal or challenge decisions based on data. These choices shape not only policies, but also public trust in institutions and in the role of data in civic life.

Bringing it together

Across workplaces and public institutions, data literacy is about shared judgment. It shows up in how workers interpret the data that they encounter, how leaders frame questions and evaluate models, how educators support learners, and how public officials communicate decisions.

As responsibility increases, so do stakes and consequences. Yet the underlying habits remain familiar: noticing patterns, questioning sources, comparing alternatives, asking for clarification, and communicating with honesty and respect. Data literacy makes it easier for people at every level to work together, understand trade-offs, and improve systems over time.

TEN

Data in Technical and Digital Systems Roles

People in technical and digital systems roles work with systems, software, processes, and technologies that create, collect, process, and act on data. They design, operate, and maintain digital systems that record activity, measure conditions, move information between systems, turn input data into results (including automated actions), and deliver those results to people and other systems. Their choices influence reliability, efficiency, user experience, privacy, and trust. These roles span three broad groups:

- Software and Systems Roles
- Data and Analytical Roles
- Governance, Privacy, and Compliance Roles

Figure 14. Technical Roles Shape how Data Flows and how it Affects People

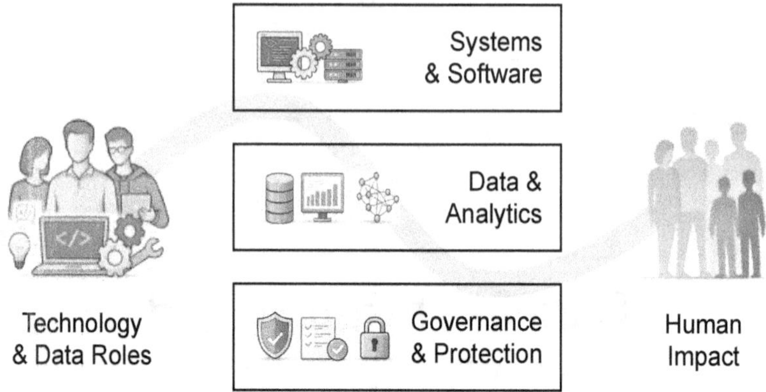

Each group focuses on a different part of this work. Yet, all depend on shared data literacy: understanding how data is generated, how it flows through systems, and how it is shaped into representations, predictions, and results. Everyone in these roles must be aware of how those results shape decisions, experiences, outcomes, and human impacts.

Software and systems roles

People working in software and systems roles design, build, and operate the digital environments where data is created, collected, stored, and processed. Examples include software and systems engineers, operations teams that keep systems running, product managers who guide what gets built, specialists who manage access and security, and designers and researchers who study how people actually use digital tools. They encounter data through:

- System records such as logs, traces, and events
- Transactions and changes in system state
- Configuration settings and feature controls
- Performance and reliability measurements
- Tickets, incidents, and service histories
- User research, usability observations, and feedback

Data literacy in these roles involves reading signals from running systems. Logs and measurements reveal performance, failures, and usage patterns. Events and transactions show how requests move through different parts of a system. Interpreting these signals requires framing questions such as: *What changed? When? For whom? Over what time window?*

These roles also manage ongoing system changes. Software updates and feature rollouts generate data that helps assess impact. System literacy blends engineering judgment with interpretation, distinguishing noise from signal and routine variation from real incidents.

These roles shape privacy and trust through implementation choices: what information is recorded, how long it is kept, how sensitive fields are protected, and how permissions and defaults guide behavior. Technical design decisions are also data decisions; they determine who can do what, under what conditions, and with what consequences.

User experience roles highlight aspects of system use that numbers alone cannot capture. Usability studies, interviews, and direct observation show where confusion, friction, or unmet needs arise. Bringing these observations together with quantitative measures supports better decisions about features, defaults, accessibility, and consent.

Data and analytics roles

People in data and analytics roles focus on turning data into information that others can understand and use. These roles prepare data, look for patterns, test ideas, and support learning from data generated by activities and systems. Examples include data engineers, analytics engineers, analysts, data scientists, and machine-learning engineers. They work with many kinds of data, such as:

- Records and files created by systems and applications
- Logs, transactions, and data streams describing event sequences
- Text, images, or other unstructured content
- Definitions, categories, and reference information
- Summaries, comparisons, and trend reports
- Forecasts, scores, and other predictions
- Experiments and evaluation dashboards

Both operational data and analytical data matter in this work. Operational data describes what is happening, such as requests, sessions, transactions, and events as systems run. Analytical data organizes that activity into summaries and patterns like totals, averages, segments, trends, and projections. Understanding how these views connect helps ensure that analysis reflects reality.

Data is created with purpose. Purpose guides use.

Data literacy in these roles starts with understanding how data is created. Data fields reflect decisions made by people and systems. Categories and definitions shape what can be compared. Data may be incomplete, delayed, or influenced by changing rules and practices. Recognizing these conditions helps prevent overconfident conclusions based on misunderstood or partial information.

Some analytical work involves statistical techniques or artificial intelligence. AI systems, in particular, are increasingly used to classify information, recommend actions, and make predictions. Literacy here looks beyond how these systems work, to understand how their outputs are evaluated, monitored, and used. Results need to be checked over time, across groups, and in real situations where decisions affect people.

Communication is a core responsibility in these roles. People working with data and analysis translate findings into implications for products, operations, policies, or services. Being clear about assumptions, uncertainty, and limits builds trust and supports better decisions. In practice, careful explanation often matters more than technical sophistication.

Governance, privacy, and compliance roles

Governance, privacy, and compliance roles establish and maintain the rules that make data use safe, lawful, and responsible. Examples include data governance and stewardship, information security, privacy and policy specialists, and risk, audit, and compliance roles. They encounter data through:

- Policies, standards, and retention schedules
- Classification schemes and access controls
- Privacy reviews and risk assessments
- Regulatory requirements and audit results
- Data use cases and exception requests
- Breach reports and incident investigations

Data literacy blends policy with practical understanding. Governance functions need to know how data moves through systems, who depends on it, where it accumulates, and where it becomes sensitive. Privacy decisions examine purpose, minimization, and proportionality. Security decisions examine access, authentication, and potential misuse.

These roles rely on dialogue with technical teams. Policies that ignore system realities become unenforceable; systems that ignore policy create risk. Shared literacy makes rules both principled and workable.

Working together across the roles

It isn't practical for these technical and digital systems roles to operate independently. Software depends on data; models depend on systems; governance depends on both; and both depend on governance. Collaboration benefits from:

- Shared definitions of events, transactions, users, and outcomes
- Shared understanding of where data originates and how it changes
- Shared framing of uncertainty, risk, and confidence
- Shared accountability for privacy, safety, and rights

Disagreements may arise from mismatches in assumptions about what is being measured, who is included, frequency of data updates, and what success means. Data literacy provides the vocabulary and reasoning needed to surface and resolve these mismatches.

Human impact and responsibility

Digital systems influence how people work, learn, and receive services. They shape defaults and incentives, and sometimes automate decisions. Privacy, fairness, accessibility, and explainability should be built into systems.

Data decisions affect real people and lives.

Governance anchors responsibility. Classification schemes protect sensitive information. Access controls prevent misuse. Data minimization reduces exposure. Retention schedules limit accumulation. Documentation clarifies the purpose. Appeal and override mechanisms preserve agency.

When technical and digital systems roles embrace data literacy as contextual, ethical, and communicative, rather than only analytical, they help ensure that data and automated systems serve human well-being. And they become part of wider practices in which individuals, families, organizations, and communities all have a role in questioning, interpreting, and shaping how data influences daily life.

PART IV

Data Literacy
Knowledge and Practice

Data literacy develops through practice. It takes shape in daily routines, conversations, decisions, and reflections. By this point in the book, the settings have changed many times—home, school, work, community, leadership, public life—but the habits have remained steady.

This final part gathers those habits together.

Data literacy is a set of recurring practices: counting and measuring, classifying and comparing, noticing patterns and change, asking careful questions, and turning information into insight. These practices shape how people interpret information and how they act on what they see.

Chapter 11 focuses on the everyday habits that support data literacy. These habits are practical and portable. They show up in small moments, such as when reading a headline, reviewing a bill, interpreting a chart, or questioning a claim. Over time, repeated use turns these habits into steady judgment.

Chapter 12 steps back to consider how these practices mature across a lifetime. Data literacy becomes part of how a person sees, thinks, learns, connects, and grows. Curiosity sustains it. Experience deepens it. Reflection strengthens it.

Together, these chapters move from technique to orientation— from what people do with data to how they live with data. The goal is steady practice, thoughtful engagement, and lifelong curiosity in a world where information never stops arriving.

Everyday Habits of Data Literacy

Working with data begins with ordinary human habits. Across history and across cultures, people have counted, sorted, compared, and observed patterns. They tracked seasons, stored grain, measured land, recorded debts, and watched the sky for signs of change. Today's tools are more sophisticated, yet the underlying moves remain familiar.

Figure 15. From Measurement to Meaning

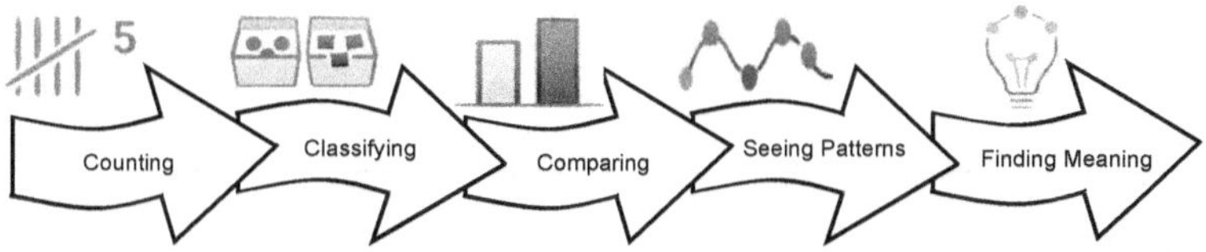

Counting and measuring

Counting is the simplest way to transform experience into information: *How many? How often? How much?*

Counting creates a record that can be revisited. Measuring adds units—dollars, minutes, miles, degrees, percentages—so quantities can be compared across time and situations. People count steps walked, hours worked, tickets in queue, students present, and votes cast. They measure temperature, blood pressure, revenue, response time, and air quality. These actions bring clarity. They allow experience to be described in consistent terms.

> *Useful counts define what is being counted*
> *and how it is measured.*

Every measurement highlights certain aspects of reality and leaves others in the background. When we count steps, we focus on movement. When we measure revenue, we focus on income. When we measure attendance, we focus on presence. Measurement sharpens focus while narrowing scope. Working well with data means recognizing both the clarity and the limits that measurement creates.

Classifying and categorizing

Once things are counted, they are often sorted. Categories organize complexity and guide decisions. Items become approved or pending, on time or late, low or high risk. Students may be grouped by reading level. Hospitals may classify cases by urgency.

Retailers sort products by department. Categories support coordination. They reduce ambiguity and make action easier.

Categories also reflect human judgment. Someone defines where boundaries sit and what qualifies for each label. A cutoff score separates passing from failing. A threshold distinguishes routine from urgent. Once established, these lines feel natural because they are used repeatedly.

People define categories.
Categories influence how data is seen and used.

Data literacy includes comfort with classification and awareness of its influence. It encourages attention to how categories are defined, how consistently they are applied, and how they shape outcomes.

Comparing and contrasting

Comparison gives numbers perspective. A value gains meaning when observed in relationship to other numbers. *Is this higher or lower? Faster or slower? More or less?*

Scales give context to numbers. They describe the range of values that a number may have. For example, a score of 78 takes on a different meaning depending on the scale. On a test graded from 0 to 100, 78 might represent solid performance. On a scale of 0 to

80, it would be near the top. On a scale of 0 to 1,000, it would be very low. The same number can carry different meanings depending on its range.

Temperature works the same way. A reading of 40 degrees makes sense only when we know whether it is measured in Fahrenheit or Celsius. Forty degrees Fahrenheit feels cold; forty degrees Celsius signals extreme heat. Understanding the unit and range is the first step toward understanding the number.

Once the scale is clear, comparison deepens the meaning. A temperature reading becomes informative when viewed against typical conditions. Forty degrees Fahrenheit may feel mild in winter and unusually cool in summer. A ten percent increase may seem dramatic until we see the starting point. A household expense of $500 means something different depending on income, prior spending, and expectations.

Comparison highlights differences in degree.
Contrast highlights differences in kind or structure.

Comparison focuses on the degree of difference in numbers. It asks how much more, how much less, how far apart. Contrast focuses on the difference in kind or pattern. It highlights distinctions that shape interpretation. Two neighborhoods may have similar average incomes but differ sharply in their age distributions. Two students may earn the same score yet arrive there through different strengths. Two stores may generate equal revenue but rely on very different customer bases. Contrasting helps reveal structure beneath surface similarity.

Thoughtful comparing and contrasting align definitions, time frames, and groups. They ensure that like is measured against like and that meaningful differences are clearly recognized. When scales differ, categories shift, or baselines move, interpretation becomes unstable even if the numbers themselves are accurate.

Together, comparison and contrast provide perspective. They help locate a number within a broader picture and clarify what is similar, what is different, and why those differences matter.

Patterns, relationships, and trends

Individual numbers offer snapshots. Patterns reveal structure.

A pattern appears when something repeats, groups, or behaves in a recognizable way. It may show up as a rhythm, a cluster, or a tendency. Some patterns are visible in space, such as certain neighborhoods having more trees or more traffic. Others appear in behavior, such as weekend spending regularly exceeding weekday spending. Some patterns reveal relationships between two things that seem to move together.

Patterns describe connection. Trends describe direction.

Relationships are a special kind of pattern. They suggest a connection. When one thing changes, another often changes as well. For example:

- As screen time increases late at night, sleep quality often declines.
- As customer wait times increase, satisfaction scores tend to fall.
- As outdoor temperatures rise, electricity use for air conditioning increases.

These examples do not automatically imply cause. They reveal an association: a pattern that invites deeper thinking. Recognizing relationships encourages questions: *Why do these move together? What else might influence both?*

Trends are patterns that unfold across time. They show direction, including steady growth, gradual decline, seasonal fluctuations, and recurring cycles. A rising grocery bill over several months suggests something different from a single expensive week. A steady improvement in reading scores tells a different story than one unusually high result.

Patterns and trends often work together. For example, a business might notice a trend of increasing sales across the year. At the same time, it may see a recurring seasonal pattern, such as higher sales in December and lower sales in February. Looking at both together gives a fuller picture. One shows direction over time; the other shows recurring structure within that time.

Or consider personal health. A person may observe a long-term trend toward better fitness while also noticing a weekly pattern: energy dips every Thursday. The trend shows progress. The pattern reveals rhythm. Both matter.

Working with patterns requires patience and attention to context. One data point rarely establishes structure. Repetition strengthens confidence. Seeing a relationship in one setting invites checking whether it appears elsewhere. Observing a trend encourages watching whether it continues.

Patterns invite exploration. Relationships invite explanation. Trends invite reflection about direction and change. Together, they help people move beyond isolated numbers toward a deeper understanding.

Finding meaning and making sense

Counting, sorting, comparing, contrasting, and observing patterns all create information. That information serves a larger purpose: understanding. Information is the raw material that is used to find meaning. Meaning develops when information connects to a question. *What does this suggest? Why might this be happening? How does this fit with what I already know? What might this mean for what we do next?*

Sense-making begins by bringing earlier observations together. A number is counted. It is placed on a scale. It is compared to other values. A pattern or relationship is observed. Then interpretation begins.

For example, a family may notice that grocery spending has risen steadily over several months. Counting reveals the total. Comparison shows the increase. A pattern emerges across time. Meaning develops when they ask why. *Is food more expensive? Are buying habits changing? Are more meals being eaten at home?* Each possibility suggests a different response.

At work, a team might see that customer complaints increase on certain days. The numbers alone show frequency. A pattern reveals timing. Sense-making requires looking deeper: *Are those days understaffed? Do they follow a promotion? Do they coincide with delivery delays?* Understanding grows when relationships are recognized and explored.

In community life, a chart might show that housing costs are rising faster than incomes. Comparison reveals the gap. A trend shows direction. Meaning develops when people consider who is affected, what trade-offs exist, and what actions are possible.

Sense-making blends evidence, context, and experience. It invites explanation and avoids blind reaction. It requires curiosity, patience, and conversation.

Two people can look at the same information and reach different interpretations. Differences often arise from varied assumptions, priorities, or experiences. Explaining reasoning clearly strengthens shared understanding. Listening to alternative interpretations expands perspective.

Insight often arrives gradually. It may clarify a recurring expense, reveal a hidden bottleneck, or explain why two groups experience the same situation differently. Insight connects information to action in a way that feels coherent and grounded.

Information is abundant. Meaning grows through thoughtful interpretation. Insight develops when understanding influences decisions in a steady, responsible way.

Sense-making is where data literacy becomes personal. It transforms tools into judgment and information into understanding.

Curious thinking, cautious thinking, and critical thinking

Information is constantly present in daily life, and thoughtful data literacy begins with a simple habit: pause and think before responding. The tools and techniques described earlier, like counting, comparing, contrasting, and recognizing patterns, gain strength when guided by sound judgment. Three habits help guide that judgment: curiosity, caution, and critical reflection.

Pause. Think. Ask.
Careful thought guides good judgment.
Good judgment shapes data interpretation.

Each of these habits includes a quiet but powerful question: *What don't I know? What might I be missing? What else should I ask?* Recognizing the limits of what we know often strengthens understanding as much as the information itself.

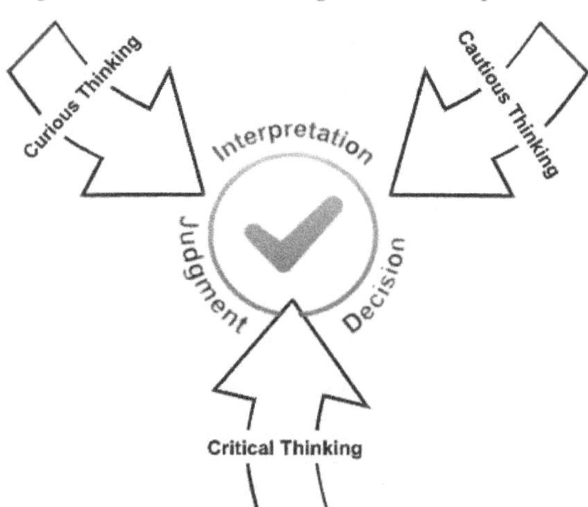

Figure 16. Habits of Thinking for Data Interpretation

Curious thinking begins with interest. It asks questions before drawing conclusions. When a number stands out, curiosity creates the pause that prevents immediate and uninformed reaction. *Why did this change? What else might be happening? Is there more beneath the surface?*

Curiosity turns data into exploration. A parent noticing higher grocery bills may wonder whether prices rose, preferences changed, or schedules shifted. A teacher observing uneven participation may ask whether timing, topic, or format influenced engagement. A manager reviewing performance data may explore whether recent changes in staffing or policy influenced results. Curiosity keeps interpretation open. It allows space for multiple possibilities and encourages learning before judging.

Curiosity turns data into exploration,
and information into understanding.

Cautious thinking adds steadiness. It slows interpretation just enough to consider limits and context. When a result looks dramatic, caution checks the scale. When two values differ, caution examines whether the comparison is fair. When a pattern appears, caution looks for repetition before declaring a conclusion.

Caution protects against overconfidence. A single strong month of sales does not guarantee a long-term trend. One survey may not represent an entire community. A sudden dip may reflect timing, weather, or reporting delays. Caution also applies to systems that generate scores and predictions. Recommendations and automated outputs may feel precise. Cautious thinking asks how those outputs were generated, what data they rely on, and where judgment still matters.

Critical thinking brings evaluation. It weighs explanations and considers evidence. It asks which interpretation best fits the information available and what additional information would strengthen understanding.

Critical thinking connects patterns to reasoning. If two measures move together, it asks what relationship might explain that connection. If groups experience the same process differently, it explores underlying conditions to find deeper meaning than shown in surface numbers.

Critical thinking also invites revision. When new evidence appears, earlier conclusions can be adjusted. Growth comes from refining interpretation over time.

These three habits reinforce one another. Curiosity opens questions. Caution stabilizes interpretation. Critical thinking strengthens explanation. Together, they support thoughtful engagement with information across personal, professional, and public life.

When these habits become routine, working with data feels less like technical work and more like informed judgment. They help transform information into understanding and understanding into wise action.

From information to insight

Data surrounds us. Data becomes information through thinking and interpretation. Information provides insight through attention and reflection.

Information includes numbers, categories, patterns, summaries, and reports. By itself, information records what has been observed or measured. Meaning begins to form when that information is placed in context. A number on a page becomes meaningful when we understand its scale, its comparison points, and the situation in which it appears.

Understanding grows when pieces begin to fit together. Patterns connect with explanations. Relationships clarify how different factors move together. Trends show direction. Patterns and trends that fit together help to create a clear picture of the world represented by data.

Insight grows from understanding. Insight appears when that clearer picture reshapes how we see a situation and influences what we choose to do next. It brings focus. It clarifies what matters and why.

Meaning drives understanding.
Understanding drives insight.

A leader who recognizes a staffing bottleneck gains an understanding of workflow. Insight appears when that understanding leads to adjustments in scheduling. A family that identifies a spending pattern develops an understanding of its habits. Insight emerges when that understanding prompts new choices. A community that recognizes a housing trend expands their understanding of local conditions. Insight appears when that kind of understanding shapes policy direction.

Insight grows through connection. It connects numbers to context, patterns to explanation, and relationships to lived conditions. It links what is measured to what is experienced.

Often insight develops gradually. A pattern becomes clearer through repetition. A relationship gains strength when seen across situations. A trend gains confidence when it continues consistently. Through reflection and conversation, interpretation sharpens and perspective widens.

Insight influences action because it clarifies what matters. Curiosity broadens exploration. Caution strengthens interpretation. Critical reflection refines conclusions. The question *What might I be missing?* continues to strengthen judgment even after understanding grows.

Working with data reaches its purpose here. Numbers become meaning. Meaning becomes understanding. Understanding becomes insight. Insight shapes how we respond. That progression turns information into informed action—and habit into lasting capability.

Twelve

A Lifetime of Curiosity and Discovery

Data literacy grows across the course of life. It deepens as roles shift and experience accumulates. Habits formed in early encounters with numbers and information continue to develop through school, work, family life, and civic participation. Across these stages, information becomes meaning, meaning becomes understanding, and understanding becomes insight.

This steady progression shapes how people approach information and how they move from understanding to action.

Data literacy develops through practice.

Figure 17. Data Literacy as a Way of Seeing, Thinking, Learning, Connecting, and Growing

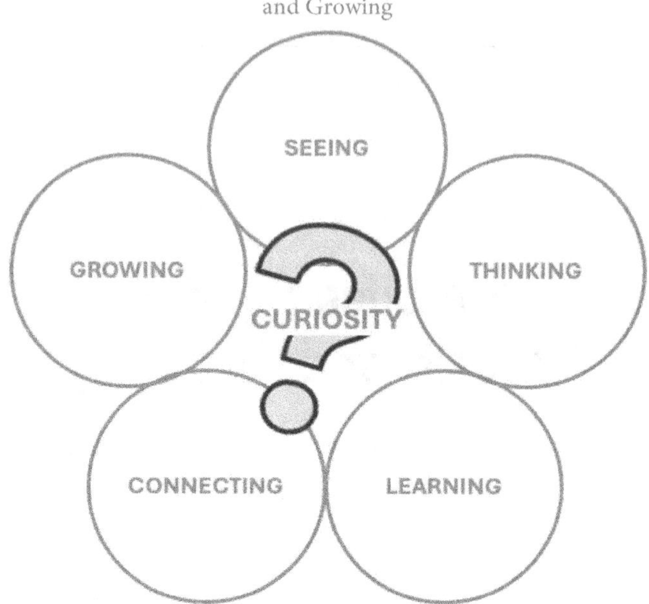

A way of seeing

Data literacy begins with awareness. It changes how information is noticed and how the world is interpreted.

A chart becomes more than an image. A headline becomes more than a statement. A number becomes more than a figure on a page. Each reflects choices: what to measure, how to categorize, which comparisons to make, and which patterns to highlight. Seeing with data means recognizing those choices.

When looking at the world through data,
understand the choices made to
collect, examine, interpret, and present the data.

It also means understanding that data is one way of seeing among several. People learn through direct experience, observation, conversation, story, and memory. Data adds another lens. It organizes experience into patterns, scale, and comparison. It can confirm what we sense. It can challenge what we assume. It can reveal connections that remain invisible in daily observation.

Data is only one lens for seeing the world.
It must work together with
experience, observation, and storytelling.

Sometimes data leads the way. A report shows rising costs, and attention turns to household habits. A performance dashboard reveals uneven outcomes, and closer observation follows. At other times, experience comes first. A change in mood, energy, or behavior prompts questions. Data then helps clarify, confirm, or explain what has already been noticed.

Seeing with data means noticing what stays constant and consistent, and what shifts over time. It includes recognizing relationships between conditions that might otherwise seem unrelated. Rising prices, changing weather patterns, shifting attendance, or evolving habits become understandable when attention is structured and comparisons are deliberate.

This way of seeing strengthens clarity. It brings focus to scale, comparison, pattern, and trend. It allows scattered information to form structure and direction.

Over a lifetime, this orientation becomes instinctive. Patterns stand out quickly. Comparisons become precise. Context becomes easy to recognize. Experience and evidence begin to reinforce one another. Seeing develops through practice, and practice deepens perspective.

A way of thinking

Seeing brings awareness; thinking shapes interpretation.

Data literacy influences how people reason about what they see. It strengthens the ability to pause, examine context, and weigh explanations before responding. It encourages attention to scale, fairness in comparison, and care in drawing conclusions.

Thinking with data works alongside other forms of reasoning. People rely on experience, instinct, emotion, and conversation when making decisions. These forms of judgment carry insight shaped by memory and values. Data-informed thinking adds structure. It asks how conclusions were formed, how measures were defined, and whether patterns are consistent across different circumstances.

Sometimes intuition signals that something has changed. Data helps clarify whether that signal reflects a trend or a temporary fluctuation. At other times, a report reveals a pattern that invites reflection. Experience then provides context that numbers alone cannot convey. This way of thinking encourages balance. Curiosity opens exploration. Caution examines limits. Critical reflection weighs alternative explanations and considers evidence from multiple angles. A steady question supports all three: *What else should I consider? What might I be missing?*

Thinking with data also includes recognizing uncertainty. Few situations offer complete information. Judgments develop from the best available evidence combined with experience and perspective. Openness to refinement strengthens credibility and resilience.

Over time, this way of thinking becomes part of routine judgment. Questions are clear and purposeful. Comparisons put information in perspective. Interpretations depend on evidence and experience. Practice and reflection build confidence.

Good thinking habits light the path from evidence to sound conclusions.

Thinking skills develop through repeated engagement with information. Each decision strengthens the next. Each reflection sharpens judgment. In this way, data literacy becomes part of how people reason about the world: structured, reflective, and responsive to both evidence and experience.

A way of learning

Data literacy supports learning throughout life. Each encounter with information becomes an opportunity to acquire knowledge, connect it to what is already known, and put it to use.

Learning begins when new information is noticed and examined. A result reveals something previously unseen. A pattern highlights a connection. A comparison clarifies a difference. In these moments, knowledge expands.

Knowledge rarely stands alone. It strengthens when integrated with experience and prior understanding. Information gains meaning through context. Patterns connect to explanations. Relationships link conditions that once seemed separate. As these connections form, fragmented knowledge becomes structured and coherent.

Learning also involves refinement. New evidence can confirm existing knowledge or lead us to rethink and revise it. Feedback from action sharpens interpretation. Questions lead to deeper exploration. Through this process, knowledge gains clarity and reliability.

Learning includes putting knowledge to use. Insight guides decisions. Decisions produce results. Results generate new information. This cycle strengthens both knowledge and judgment.

Knowledge grows through learning,
and learning grows through knowledge.

Across daily life, this process appears in many settings. A student gains knowledge about effective study strategies and applies them in future courses. A professional learns how seasonal patterns affect performance and adjusts their planning accordingly. A household recognizes how small expenses accumulate and adopts new routines. A community learns how demographic shifts influence local needs and revises priorities.

Learning also grows through conversation. Sharing knowledge introduces alternative perspectives. Discussion helps test interpretations and strengthen conclusions. Collaboration connects individual understanding into shared insight.

Over time, learning becomes cumulative. Knowledge builds upon knowledge. Habits of attention, interpretation, and application strengthen. The ability to move from information to meaningful action becomes smooth and seamless.

Data literacy reinforces this lifelong process. It encourages the careful acquisition of knowledge, the thoughtful integration of evidence, and the responsible application of learning to decisions and actions.

A way of connecting

Data literacy strengthens the connection by supporting shared understanding.

Information often shapes decisions that involve more than one person. Families plan budgets. Teams coordinate projects. Communities evaluate public reports. In each setting, people interpret information together.

Connection begins with clarity. When measures are defined clearly and comparisons are explained openly, conversation becomes focused and constructive. When people describe how they reached a conclusion, others can follow the reasoning and respond thoughtfully.

Data literacy encourages this transparency. It supports explaining scale, context, and evidence. It invites questions about how patterns were identified and how conclusions were formed. Shared language around information strengthens collaboration.

Connection also grows through perspective. Different experiences shape interpretation. One person may focus on cost, another on fairness, another on long-term impact. Bringing these perspectives together broadens understanding and sharpens questions.

In families, shared interpretation helps align expectations and responsibilities. In workplaces, clear communication around metrics supports coordinated action. In communities, open discussion of public indicators builds informed participation.

Connection extends beyond agreement. It includes the ability to explain differences respectfully. When people articulate the evidence behind their views, disagreement becomes structured and purposeful. The conversation shifts from assertion to reasoning.

Data literacy supports this movement. It encourages people to ask how conclusions were formed and what evidence supports them. It promotes dialogue grounded in information and guided by mutual respect.

Through connection, individual understanding expands into shared insight. Decisions reflect a collective perspective formed through shared interpretation. In this way, data literacy strengthens relationships by supporting communication, collaboration, and responsible participation wherever information shapes shared action.

A way of growing

Growth in data literacy parallels growth in other areas of life.

As people gain experience, assume new responsibilities, and take on new roles, they encounter new forms of information. Decisions involve additional factors. Questions carry broader implications.

The habits of noticing, questioning, comparing, and interpreting develop in response.

At the same time, data literacy supports growth in those roles. Careful interpretation informs professional judgment. Deliberate comparison informs financial decisions. Attention to patterns supports planning. Examination of evidence strengthens communication.

These forms of growth reinforce one another. New responsibilities bring new questions. New questions invite closer attention to information. Experience provides context for interpreting measures and patterns. Reflection strengthens judgment.

In a data-filled world, many forms of growth involve information. Career progress often depends on understanding performance measures. Financial stability depends on understanding costs and trade-offs. Civic participation depends on interpreting public information. Data literacy supports engagement in each of these areas.

Over time, knowledge connects across situations. Experience informs interpretation. Perspective guides decisions. Growth in life and growth in literacy proceed together, each strengthening the other through practice and reflection.

In this way, data literacy becomes part of how individuals develop across personal and professional stages of life.

Staying curious

Staying curious is an individual choice. Curiosity is a personal trait that strengthens with practice. Curious people ask questions. And they ask more questions. And they keep asking questions. They look at things closely, listen carefully, and remain interested.

Curiosity becomes a habit through repeated action. It shows up in small moments: pausing before reacting, asking one more question, looking for context before forming a conclusion. Over time, those small actions shape how a person thinks and learns.

Curiosity is practiced. It grows when questions are welcomed and assumptions are examined. It grows when new information is explored. Conversation strengthens it. Reflection deepens it. Experience gives it direction.

Curious people stay engaged with the world around them. They seek to understand how things work and why they change. They look for patterns. They consider alternative explanations. They remain open to learning in both familiar and unfamiliar situations.

Curiosity supports growth in knowledge. It encourages continued learning across stages of life. It connects ideas across contexts. It sustains attention when information feels complex or uncertain. It keeps the mind active and responsive.

In a data-filled world, curiosity carries special value. Information appears constantly: numbers, charts, headlines, summaries, and forecasts. Curiosity turns that steady flow into opportunity. It asks what the information means, how it was formed, and what it suggests about action. It acts as a catalyst for change. Discovery and innovation often begin with a question overlooked by others.

Curiosity sustains data literacy across a lifetime.

Curiosity does not fade with age or experience. It can deepen over time. Each question strengthens it. Each discovery reinforces it. Each reflection renews it. Across a lifetime, curiosity sustains data literacy. It keeps us attentive, thinking disciplined, learning active, connecting respectful, and growing purposeful.

Curiosity transforms information into inquiry, inquiry into understanding, and understanding into insight. It is the steady companion of a life lived thoughtfully in a data-filled world.

Continuing the journey

Throughout this book, data literacy has been described as a way of seeing, thinking, learning, connecting, growing, and staying curious. These are habits that individuals bring into everyday life.

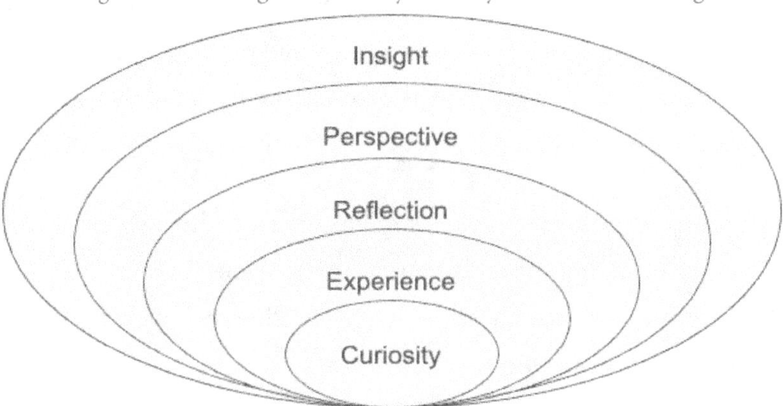

Figure 18. Growing Data Literacy: The Layers of Understanding

Data literacy makes a difference wherever information influences choice.

Information shapes daily routines and long-term plans. It informs financial decisions, workplace responsibilities, health choices, and civic participation. Each encounter with information offers an opportunity to apply attention, judgment, and curiosity.

The progression remains steady. Information gains meaning in context. Meaning develops into understanding as patterns and relationships connect. Understanding becomes insight when it guides action. Action generates new information, and the cycle continues.

Curiosity sustains that movement. Questions invite exploration. Evidence invites examination. Reflection invites learning. Over time, these habits shape how a person engages with information and how that person engages with the world.

In a data-filled world, individuals who cultivate data literacy participate with awareness and responsibility. They communicate with clarity. They make decisions anchored in evidence and experience. They approach uncertainty with steady judgment.

The journey continues in ordinary moments, such as when a claim invites examination, when a pattern invites reflection, and when a decision invites careful thought. Data literacy lives in those moments for those who practice it.

Across a lifetime, the habits described here remain valuable. They travel through changing roles, responsibilities, and circumstances.

The work continues. The questions continue. The learning continues.

Data Literacy Body of Knowledge (DLBOK)

Data literacy is both a habit of mind and a body of knowledge. Throughout this book, the emphasis has been on developing the habits that support thoughtful engagement with information. Those habits rest on understanding. The Data Literacy Body of Knowledge outlines the core domains that support informed participation in a data-filled world.

This appendix organizes the essential concepts that shape data literacy. It defines the knowledge areas that strengthen interpretation, responsibility, communication, and decision making across personal, professional, and civic contexts.

The domains presented here are interconnected. Foundations support responsibility. Responsible practices strengthen evaluation. Careful evaluation enables sound analysis. Clear analysis supports communication. Communication informs action. Action generates learning. Together, these domains describe the landscape of data literacy.

A data-literate person builds literacy through understanding key distinctions, recognizing context, asking thoughtful questions, and applying knowledge with judgment. The domains that follow describe that understanding.

Domain 1: Foundations of data

Data literacy begins with understanding what data is and how it represents the world. Data describes the real world as recorded descriptions in the form of numbers, categories, labels, measurements, and observations that represent events, objects, and conditions. To work well with data, a person must understand how it is defined, structured, and shaped by context.

This domain establishes the fundamental concepts that make interpretation possible. It includes the nature of data, the kinds of data commonly encountered, the ways data is organized, and the importance of definitions, scale, and documentation. Without these foundations, interpretation becomes guesswork. With them, information can be examined with clarity and confidence.

A data-literate person understands:
- Data is a representation of events, objects, or conditions—not the events, objects, or conditions themselves.

- The difference between data and information, and how context gives data meaning.
- The distinction between quantitative and qualitative data.
- The role of categorical values, identifiers, and numerical measures.
- The difference between event data (what happened) and reference data (what describes or classifies).
- The distinction between structured, semi-structured, and unstructured data.
- How data is organized into records, fields, tables, and files.
- How relationships among data elements influence interpretation.
- How units of measure, timeframes, and definitions shape results.
- Why scale and granularity matter when examining information.
- The importance of metadata, which is documentation that explains how data was defined, collected, and structured.
- That changes in definition or classification can alter conclusions.

Domain 2: Data management and responsibility

Data is part of a broad information environment. It is collected, stored, shared, protected, and used within systems and communities. Every dataset reflects choices: what to measure, how to define it, who can access it, and how it may be used. Understanding these choices is part of data literacy.

This domain addresses the responsibilities that accompany working with data. It includes awareness of documentation, governance, privacy, ethics, and appropriate use. A data-literate person recognizes that data carries implications beyond analysis. Decisions about collection, protection, interpretation, and sharing influence trust, fairness, and outcomes in everyday life.

A data-literate person understands:
- Data is shaped by policies, roles, and shared responsibilities.
- Metadata provides essential context for interpreting data accurately.
- Clear definitions and documentation support consistency and trust.
- Data governance establishes guidelines for protection, quality, and appropriate use.
- Privacy considerations influence how data should be collected, stored, and shared.
- Some data is sensitive and requires heightened care.

- Fairness and bias can appear in both data and the systems that use it.
- Automated systems reflect design choices and embedded assumptions.
- Transparency strengthens credibility and informed decision making.
- Responsible use of data includes questioning limitations and potential unintended consequences.
- Every participant in a data ecosystem shares responsibility for thoughtful use.

This domain reinforces that data literacy includes stewardship. It includes both the ability to interpret information, and awareness that data affects people, communities, and decisions in meaningful ways.

Domain 3: Finding, evaluating, and preparing data

Data literacy involves more than interpreting information that appears in front of us. It includes the ability to identify what information is needed, locate appropriate sources, evaluate credibility and relevance, and prepare data for meaningful use. Before patterns are analyzed or conclusions are drawn, careful attention must be given to the quality and suitability of the data itself.

This domain focuses on thoughtful preparation. It includes framing questions clearly, identifying reliable sources, examining definitions and assumptions, and ensuring that comparisons are fair. A data-literate person understands that insight depends on the integrity of the information used to support it.

A data-literate person understands:

- Clear questions guide effective use of data.
- The purpose of analysis should be defined before gathering information.
- Data can come from many sources, including internal records, public data, surveys, and digital systems.
- The credibility of a source affects the reliability of conclusions.
- Timeliness influences whether data reflects current conditions.
- Definitions and collection methods influence comparability.
- Missing values, inconsistencies, and errors can distort interpretation.
- Preparing data may involve cleaning, aligning formats, clarifying definitions, or documenting assumptions.
- Fair comparison requires alignment in units, timeframe, and scope.
- Transparency in how data is prepared strengthens trust and understanding.

This domain emphasizes disciplined preparation. Careful framing, thoughtful evaluation, and clear documentation strengthen every subsequent step in analysis and decision making.

Domain 4: Analyzing and interpreting data

Analysis involves examining data to identify patterns, relationships, differences, and trends. Interpretation goes a step further. It asks what those observations mean and how they connect to real-world conditions. Together, analysis and interpretation transform information into understanding.

This domain addresses the habits of mind that support careful reasoning. It includes describing data accurately, making fair comparisons, recognizing patterns over time, exploring possible relationships, and acknowledging limits. A data-literate person understands that interpretation requires judgment. Evidence must be weighed, context considered, and conclusions held with appropriate confidence.

A data-literate person understands:
- Describing data clearly is the foundation for interpretation.
- Counts, totals, averages, and ranges summarize information in useful ways.
- Fair comparisons require alignment in scale, units, definitions, and timeframe.

- Relative and absolute differences can tell different stories.
- Patterns reveal repetition or consistency.
- Trends indicate direction over time.
- Relationships between measures suggest possible connections but do not automatically imply causes.
- Correlation does not establish cause.
- Variability and distribution influence how data should be interpreted.
- Uncertainty is common and should be acknowledged.
- Limited samples, incomplete data, or changing definitions can affect conclusions.
- Interpretation benefits from curiosity, caution, and critical reflection.

This domain reinforces disciplined reasoning. It encourages moving carefully from evidence to explanation, recognizing both what data reveals and where its limits remain.

Domain 5: Visualization and communication

Data gains influence when it is shared. Tables, charts, summaries, and narratives shape how others understand information. Good data visualization is done with purpose. It is a way to organize attention, highlight patterns, and clarify comparisons. Communication completes the movement from analysis to shared understanding.

This domain addresses how information is presented, interpreted, and explained. It includes choosing appropriate visual forms, recognizing how design influences perception, and communicating findings responsibly. A data-literate person understands that clarity, accuracy, and transparency are essential when sharing information with others.

A data-literate person understands:
- The purpose of a visualization should match the question being addressed.
- Visualizations typically illustrate comparisons, proportions, distributions, relationships, and trends over time.
- Different chart types are suited to different purposes, and the relationship between chart type and purpose influences clarity.
- Tables are appropriate when precise values matter.
- Visual scale influences interpretation.
- Labels, units, and context are essential for clarity.
- Design choices can emphasize or distort patterns.
- Changes in scale, truncated axes, exaggerated aspect ratios, or selective framing can create misleading impressions.
- Omitting context can mislead even when numbers are accurate.
- Clear explanations strengthen trust and understanding.
- Communication should acknowledge limits and uncertainty.

- Audience perspective influences how information is received.
- Responsible communication avoids exaggeration and selective presentation.

This domain reinforces that data literacy includes both reading and creating visual information. The ability to communicate findings clearly and responsibly strengthens informed dialogue across personal, professional, and civic life.

Domain 6: From insight to action

Data literacy reaches its full expression when understanding informs decisions. Insight exists to inform decisions. It shapes choices, guides priorities, and influences behavior across personal, professional, and civic life. When used thoughtfully, data supports informed judgment.

This domain focuses on applying understanding responsibly. It includes integrating evidence with experience, weighing tradeoffs, recognizing limits, and learning from results. A data-literate person understands that action creates new information. Decisions generate outcomes, outcomes provide feedback, and feedback strengthens future judgment.

A data-literate person understands:
- Insight connects evidence to decisions.
- Data informs judgment but does not replace it.

- Decisions often combine measurable inputs with experience, values, and context.
- Tradeoffs are common and should be considered openly.
- Outcomes should be monitored to understand the impact.
- Measures may need adjustment as conditions change.
- Feedback supports learning and improvement.
- New information may refine or revise earlier conclusions.
- Responsible action includes acknowledging uncertainty.
- Curiosity sustains continued learning after decisions are made.

This domain reinforces that data literacy extends beyond analysis. It includes informed action and thoughtful adaptation. Insight guides decisions, and decisions generate learning. Through this cycle, data literacy strengthens over time.

Glossary of Data Literacy Terms

Accuracy. How close data is to the truth it is supposed to represent. Accurate records correctly reflect what actually happened, such as a bill showing the real amount owed and paid, not a typo or outdated balance.

Aggregated statistics. Numbers that combine many individual records into summaries such as totals, averages, or percentages. For example, "average commute time in the city" is an aggregated statistic built from many people's trips, not just one.

Algorithm. A set of rules or step-by-step instructions that a computer follows to reach a result. Recommendation systems, spam filters, and price calculators all rely on algorithms that turn inputs (data) into outputs (suggestions, scores, or decisions).

Analytical data. Information that has been copied or prepared specifically for looking at patterns, trends, and comparisons over time. It is less about running today's transactions and more about questions like *How has this changed over the last year?* or *Which group is growing fastest?* (Also see **Operational data.**)

Assumption. Something treated as true without being fully proven or tested. Assumptions shape how data is collected, labeled, and interpreted, such as deciding that a "late" payment means more than seven days past the due date.

Average. A single number that summarizes the middle of a group of numbers. Averages can be calculated in different ways (for example, by adding all values and dividing by the number of items, or by giving some values more influence than others in a weighted average). Each approach will tell a different story about the same group.

Bias. A built-in tilt or slant that favors some outcomes, groups, or explanations over others. Bias can come from where data was collected, how questions were asked, who was included, or from our own tendency to notice evidence that agrees with what we already believe.

Calibration. The process of checking and adjusting a tool or system so its measurements match a trusted standard. We calibrate things like scales, thermometers, and sensors to keep their readings accurate over time.

Categorical data. Information that places things into named groups instead of measuring them with numbers. Examples include eye color, type of job, or "yes/no" responses. The categories are labels, not amounts. (See also **Classification / Category.**)

Cause. A factor that directly helps produce an outcome. Showing cause requires more than noticing that two things move together; it involves evidence and reasoning that rule out other explanations, like season, coincidence, or missing information.

Classification / Category. The act of grouping things based on shared rules or labels. Report cards, risk levels ("low," "medium," "high"), and shipping statuses ("in transit," "delivered") are all classifications that simplify complex details into action-friendly groups. (See also **Categorical data.**)

Comparison. Looking at two or more values side by side to see how they differ or resemble each other. Comparisons can highlight changes (this month vs. last month), differences between groups (store A vs. store B), or how something fits into a larger picture (one household vs. the city average).

Context. The surrounding details that give data its meaning, such as time period, location, definitions, and purpose. A temperature of 40 degrees means something very different in Celsius than in Fahrenheit; context is what tells you which one you are seeing.

Correlation. A pattern where two things move together in some way, such as both going up or down at the same time. Correlation signals association, not cause; ice cream sales and swimming both rise in summer, but buying ice cream does not cause swimming accidents.

Critical thinking. A careful way of reasoning that tests conclusions and claims instead of accepting them at face value. It involves asking where information came from, what might be missing, how else it could be explained, and what evidence would change your mind.

Curiosity. A steady desire to understand how and why things happen. In data literacy, curiosity shows up as questions such as *What is this number really telling me?* and *What else might explain this pattern?* and leads to deeper, less automatic interpretations.

Data. Recorded information that stands in for real events, objects, or conditions. Receipts, check-in times, scores, click counts, and test results are all data. They are traces real-world events that can be stored, shared, and examined later.

Data governance. The shared rules and practices that guide how data is collected, protected, and used. It covers who can see what, how quality is maintained, how privacy is respected, and who is accountable when something goes wrong.

Data literacy. The ability to read, interpret, question, communicate, and use data in thoughtful ways. It includes everyday skills like understanding charts in the news, questioning a statistic in an advertisement, and using simple records to make better personal or family decisions.

Data minimization. A principle that says only the smallest reasonable amount of personal data should be collected and kept. If a service only needs your email to work, data minimization means not asking for your birthdate, home address, or other personal data not specifically needed.

Data quality. How well data fits the job it is being used for. High-quality data is accurate, complete, timely, and consistent enough to support fair and reliable decisions; poor-quality data can mislead, even when the numbers look precise.

Decision making (data-informed). Choosing between options by combining data with experience, values, and practical limits. Data can guide decisions about budgets, staffing, or health, but it does not replace judgment; it is one voice in the discussion, not the only one.

Definition (specifically, data definition). A clear explanation of what a term, category, or measure means in a particular context. Definitions decide who counts as "employed," what qualifies as "on time," or where the cutoff is between "low" and "high" risk, and therefore shape the numbers that follow.

Distribution. The way values are spread out across a set of data. A distribution shows whether most values cluster around the middle, pile up at one end, or stretch out with a few extremely high or low cases that may deserve extra attention.

Ethics (in data). The principles that guide fair and respectful use of data about people. Ethics raise questions about consent, potential harm, unequal treatment, and who benefits from data-driven decisions, especially when individuals have little control over how their data is used.

Evidence. Information used to support a claim or conclusion. Strong evidence is relevant, comes from credible sources, and is collected and interpreted in a transparent way; weak evidence is often cherry-picked, anecdotal, or too small to support broad claims.

Governance (of data). The shared rules, roles, and practices that guide how data is collected, protected, shared, and used. Good data governance clarifies who is responsible for what, who can see which information, and how problems are handled when something goes wrong.

Granularity. How detailed or "zoomed-in" data is. Daily spending totals have finer granularity than monthly totals; a street-level map has finer granularity than a city-level map. Changing granularity can reveal or hide important patterns.

Identifier. A piece of information used to tell one record or person apart from another, such as a student ID, account number, or device ID. Identifiers make it easier to link records and track history, but they also raise privacy questions.

Information. Data that has been placed in context so that it answers a question or tells us something useful. A list of numbers becomes information when we know what they measure, when they were collected, and why they matter.

Insight. A clear, useful understanding that connects data to real-world meaning and action. Insight might show why a pattern is happening and what to do next, such as discovering that certain days are consistently understaffed and adjusting schedules accordingly.

Interpretation. The process of making sense of data by linking patterns to possible explanations. Interpretation asks what the numbers might mean, how confident we should be, and what else could be going on in the background.

Metric. A specific measure chosen to track performance, status, or change over time. Examples include on-time delivery rate, average wait time, monthly spending, or test scores. Metrics are often used as scorecards and can influence behavior and priorities.

Observational data. Information collected by actively watching what happens instead of using experiments or surveys. Examples include a city counting how many people use a park, a website recording which links people click, or a teacher noting how often students ask for help.

Operational data. Information that systems use to run day-to-day activities in real time. It describes what is happening right now or very recently, such as current orders in a store, today's appointments in a clinic, or active tickets in a help desk queue. (Also see **Analytical data.**)

Pattern. A regularity or repetition in data that suggests structure. Patterns can be simple (weekend spending is always higher) or complex (certain symptoms appear together before a health event), and they invite us to look for explanations.

Population-level information. Data that describes a whole group without details of individual cases. It might summarize all residents of a city, all patients in a hospital system, or all students in a district. It is useful for seeing big patterns, but it cannot tell you details about any specific person.

Privacy. The protection of personal or sensitive information from being accessed or used in ways people did not agree to. Privacy involves choices about what to share, with whom, for how long, and under what conditions.

Proportionality (in data use). The idea that the amount and type of data collected or used should match the importance of the goal and the level of risk. A proportional approach avoids collecting more information than needed or using harsh measures for minor issues.

Qualitative data. Descriptive information that captures qualities or characteristics instead of counts, quantities, or measurements. It may appear as simple descriptions (such as color, condition, or material), as categories or labels (such as "satisfied," "neutral," and "dissatisfied"), or as longer text such as interview notes and open-ended survey responses. (Also see **Quantitative data, Categorical data.**)

Quantitative data. Information expressed in numbers that can be counted or measured, such as income, temperature, scores, or distances. Quantitative data allows calculations and numeric comparisons, but still needs context and definitions to be meaningful. (Also see **Qualitative data.**)

Record. A collection of related data about a single person, event, or item. A medical record may include visits, medications, and test results; a purchase record may include date, store, items, prices, and payment method.

Reference data. Standard lists or codes used to label, classify, or give context to other data. Examples include country codes, grade levels, or product categories; they help keep records consistent across systems.

Relationship. A connection between two or more measures or categories. For example, as wait times increase, satisfaction scores may tend to fall. Relationships suggest that things move together in some way, but do not automatically prove why.

Retention schedule. A plan that states how long data should be kept and when it should be deleted or archived. Retention schedules might say that routine logs are kept for 90 days, tax records for seven years, and certain legal records for much longer.

Risk. The chance that something harmful, costly, or unwanted will happen. In data use, risk includes making decisions with incomplete information, misinterpreting a trend, or relying too heavily on an automated score that may be biased or outdated.

Sampling. Using a smaller group to represent a larger population when collecting data. A good sample is selected carefully so its results can reasonably stand in for the whole; a poor sample can give a distorted picture that leads to misleading conclusions.

Scale (measurement). The range and units used to express a measurement. A score of 40 can mean "cold" or "extremely hot" depending on whether the scale is Fahrenheit or Celsius; knowing the scale is essential to understanding the number.

Scenario models. Structured "what if" exercises that use data and assumptions to explore possible futures. A scenario model might estimate what happens if prices rise, if demand drops, or if a new policy is introduced, helping people compare options before making decisions.

Sensitive data. Information that could cause harm, discrimination, or serious embarrassment if misused or exposed. This includes health details, financial records, precise locations, and information about children or other vulnerable groups.

Structured data. Data organized into clearly defined fields and tables, like a spreadsheet where each column has a specific meaning. Structured data is easier for software to search, sort, and analyze in standard ways.

Timeliness. How current and up-to-date data is for the purpose at hand. In some situations, a few minutes' delay matters; in others, monthly or yearly updates are enough. Old data can be misleading if conditions have changed.

Tolerance (in measurement). The small range of difference that is considered acceptable around a target value. For example, a part might be allowed to be slightly longer or shorter than its ideal length, as long as it stays within the agreed tolerance and still works properly.

Trade-off. A situation in which improving one thing usually means giving up something else. For example, stricter fraud checks may reduce false approvals but increase waiting time. Data can help clarify tradeoffs, but people must still choose priorities.

Trend. A general direction of change over time, such as steady growth, gradual decline, or repeated cycles. A single high or low point is not a trend; trends become visible when we look across many points and see a consistent pattern.

Uncertainty. Recognition that conclusions are never perfect because information, conditions, and measurements are limited. Uncertainty does not mean "know nothing"; it means being honest about how confident we can be and where caution is wise.

Variability. A measure of how much difference there is among data values. Low variability means most values are close together; high variability means they are spread out. Variability affects how much weight we give to averages or single examples.

Visualization. A picture that represents data, such as a chart, graph, or map. Good visualizations make patterns, differences, and trends easier to see at a glance, while poor or misleading ones can hide important details or exaggerate small differences.

Index